James Smith Buck

The Chronicles of the Land of Columbia

Vol. 1

James Smith Buck

The Chronicles of the Land of Columbia
Vol. 1

ISBN/EAN: 9783337293239

Printed in Europe, USA, Canada, Australia, Japan

Cover: Foto ©Thomas Meinert / pixelio.de

More available books at **www.hansebooks.com**

THE CHRONICLES,

OF THE

LAND OF COLUMBIA,

COMMONLY CALLED

AMERICA.

FROM THE LANDING OF THE PILGRIM FATHERS, TO THE SECOND REIGN OF ULYSSES THE I. A PERIOD OF TWO HUNDRED AND FIFTY-TWO YEARS.

IN WHICH IS GIVEN, A SHORT ACCOUNT OF THE SETTLEMENT OF THE COUNTRY, THE WARS WITH THE AMELAKITTS THAT FORMERLY OCCUPIED THE LAND, THE INTRODUCTION OF SLAVERY, THE FORMATION OF THE DIFFERENT POLITICAL PARTIES, IN CONSEQUENCE OF THAT, AND THE EMIGRATION TO OUR SHORES, FROM THE REALMS ACROSS THE WATERS; THE NAME OF EACH CHIEF RULER, AND HIS COUNCELORS, THE WAR OF THE REVOLUTION, OF EIGHTEEN HUNDRED AND TWELVE, AND THE GREAT REBELLION; IN ANCIENT FORM.

BY THE PROPHET JAMES.

---•---

BOOK I.

---•---

1876.
PUBLISHED BY F. W. STEARNS, 114 MICHIGAN ST.
MILWAUKEE, WIS.

THE FIRST BOOK OF THE CHRONICLES OF COLUMBIA,
A CENTENNIAL OFFERING TO HER SONS,
BY THE AUTHOR.

Entered according to act of Congress A. D. 1875, By
J. S. BUCK,
in the office of the Librarian of Congress at Washington, D. C.

In offering this Volume of Chronicles, to the Public, the Author has two objects in view; first, to gratify the large number that have desired the publication of them; and also to make some Ducats; for no man can afford to print a book (if it is a poor one) unless he is paid therefor, and who should pay, except it be those that may have been amused, or disgusted, (as the case may be) with, what is written. The subjects treated of are such as must interest every one that has the good of his country at heart, for believe me, men of America; the tendency of the Government is toward Anarchy, and disruption, which must of necessity come, from the concentration of so much wealth, and power, in the hands of the few, and the corruption that follow it, that, in connection with the jealousies arrising from the different Nationalities among us, is fast working the downfall of all political honesty, and virtue, the only one thing that can ever make a nation truly great, prosperous, and happy; and unless greater watchfulness is exercised in our national affairs, the time for our destruction will soon come, and we shall be numbered with the nations of old, that have passed away in consequence of their vices; for wealth brings power, and power corruption, and corruption political death.

Hoping that Columbia, may shun the rocks, that lie in her path, and that the Stars, and Stripes, may never cease to wave, o'er the Land of the free, and the home of the brave, is the sincere wish of

THE AUTHOR.

THE I BOOK OF THE

Chronicles of the Land of Columbia,

COMMONLY CALLED

AMERICA.

CHAPTER I.

1. There is a land called Columbia: and the same extendeth form the ocean called Atlantic, on the East, unto the great ocean called Pacific, on the West, and from the waters called Arctic, on the North, unto the Gulf called Mexico, on the South; it is an *exceeding great, and a goodly Land.*

2. And it was the abode of the *Narragansite*, the *Abenakite* the *Pequodite*, the *Pennacookite*, the *Nipmunkite*, the *Manhattanite*, and the *Mohawkite*; yea, from one extremity of the Land, unto the other, it was full, of savage beasts, and still more savage men!

3. And they had occupied the Land for long ages past, but, now; like the Cannanites of old, the cup of their iniquity was full, and the time for their destruction had come; for the seed of *Japheth* was to possess the Land.

4. And to this Land, came our Fathers, in ancient times, from the realm of Britain, (the same is called Albion, or England,) directed by the finger of God, for they said there can we worship Him, after the dictates of our own conscience, which we cannot do, here in this Land.

5. For when they would worship Him after the dictates of their own conscience, the King of the realm of Britain, did say unto them; nay, but ye shall not do this thing.

6. For like Nebuchadnezzar of old, the King of the realm of Britain, had set up an Image; in his dominions; (the same is called the established Church,) and made a decree; that whomsoever dwelt in the realm, should worship the Image, that he had set up.

7. Now there were many of the subjects of the King, that like Daniel feared not, to disobey the Decree, neither would they worship the image, that he had set up.

8. And when this was made known unto the King, it came to pass, that he was exceeding wroth, and his countenance was changed, and he sent for his chief priests, and his wise men, and

his counselors, to come before him, and when they were come into his presence, he spake unto them, after this manner.

9. What is this that I hear, that there be many of my subjects, who have set at, naught my Decree,—neither will they worship the image, that I have set up.

10. And they answered the King saying; O! King! live for ever, but be it known unto thee, that there are divers of the Baser sort, in this realm, that refuse to obey the Decree, that thou hast made, neither will they worship the Image, that thou hast set up, and these (Rebels) are called Puritans.

11. Now therefore let the King make a new Decree, and let it go forth from the Palace at White-hall, that when the people shall hear the sound of the Cornet, Flute, Harp, Sackbut, Psaltry; and all kinds of music; that then, shall they fall down, and worship the Image, that thou hast set up.

12. And that if any shall disobey the Decree of the King, then shall they be destroyed, and their goods taken for a prey, and the King made such a Decree.

13. Then were these people in great distress, and they cried mightily unto God, for help against their enemies, and he heard the

14. And he said unto them, get ye out of this land, unto a land that I shall shew thee, and I will give it unto thee, and unto thy seed after thee, unto the latest Generation, for a Possession; and he brought them to Columbia.

15. Now it came to pass, that the ship in which they were, came unto that portion of the land, that is called New England, unto a place called by the former inhabitants thereof *Patuxet* (which meaneth, that it hath no owner,) and they landed at that place.

16. And they took possession of the land, in the twelth month, on the twenty-second day of the month, in the name of God, and their dread sovereign; the King, of the realm of Britain, and they called the place, New Plymouth.

17. Now these people, were called the Pilgrim Fathers, and they were in number five score and one persons; and they commenced to build a city.

18. And they grew, and multiplied, for many came to them, yet from the realm of Britain, until they filled the Land, albeit they did not utterly drive out the former inhabitants, for they remain unto this day; but they did war against them, continually.

19. And here in this new world, did these brave men, plant the tree of Civil, and Religous Liberty, the branches whereof cover the whole Land, and the blessings of which; we their children, enjoy unto this day; Yea, and the oppressed of every land, find a home beneath its shadow.

20. And the land became a province of the realm of Britain; for although the people had been sorely oppressed in former times, still they remained loyal; to the King.

21. But at length the King so oppressed them, that they did Rebel, and after a long and bloodly war, they became free men, and this war, was called the war of the Revolution.

22. Now George, whose sir name

CHAPTER I.

was Washington, led the Hosts of Columbia against the Hosts of the King of Britain, and after the people had become free, they made George, the first chief ruler.*

23. And they gave him John, whose sir name was Adams, to go in and out, before him, and to stand in his place, in certain times; Thomas, whose sir name was Jefferson, was chief scribe over the people; Henry, whose sir name was Knox, was chief in the department of war; and Alexander whose sir name was Hamilton, was over the treasury of the people.

24. Now George, was from the Province of Virginia, and was more beloved than any other man in the land, moreover, he was called by the people, the Father of his Country, for he had delivered it, out of the hand of the King of Britain.

25. Now there was trouble in the reign of George, with the Ame-le-kites of the West Provinces, on account of the treachery, of the servants of the King of Britain.

26. But George commanded Anthony, (sir named the mad,) and he led the Hosts of Columbia against them, and discomfited them greatly, insomuch, that they troubled, the realm no more, all the days of George.

27. Likewise did the Provinces of Kentuckey, and Tennessee, became a part of the realm, in his reign; making the number of Provinces, sixteen.

28. Also, was there trouble with the realm of Gaul, (commonly called France,) in the reign of George the I,
on account of the acts of some of her servants.

29. For they sought to use the ports of the realm, as a shelter for the prizes, taken on the sea from the realm of Britain, with whom they were at war, but by the wisdom of George, and the men of the Sanhedrim, peace did prevail.

30. Now the rest of the acts of George, and all that he did, behold they are written in the book of the records of the Sanhedrim, at Washington, made during his reign.

31. And when eight years were expired, the people made John;† chief ruler in his stead, but the memory of George, shall never fade from the minds and hearts, of the people of Columbia, to the latest generation.

32. Now John the I, was also one of the mighty ones of the realm, eloquent of tongue, firm for liberty, from the Province of Massachusetts, and of the Whig party, and had aided greatly, in freeing the land, from the King of Britain.

33. And they gave him Thomas, whose sir name was Jefferson, to go in and out before him, and to stand in his place in certain times; Timothy, whose sir name was Pickering, was chief scribe over the people; James, whose sir name was McHenry, was chief in the department of war; George, whose sir name was Cabot, was over the ships of war, and Oliver, whose sir name was Wolcott, was over the treasury of the people.

34. Now there was trouble with the

---

* 1789.   † Adams. 97.

realm of Britain, in the reign of John the I, but by his wisdom, together with the men of the Sanhedrim, was the realm saved from war.

35. Also was the land smitten with a pestilence, the like of which had not been seen before in Columbia, nevertheless, it prospered greatly.

36. And John the I, reigned four years in Columbia, and peace did prevail, for he ruled with great wisdom.

37. And all his acts, and all that he did, behold they are written in the book of the records, of the Sanhedrim, at Washington, made during his reign, and the people made Thomas,‡ chief ruler, in his stead, and he commenced to reign.

---

‡ Jefferson. 1801.

CHAPTER II.

1. Now Thomas the I, was from the Province of Virginia, he also was a mighty counselor in the Sanhedrim, and he it was that framed the writing, called the Constitution, that doth govern the people of Columbia, unto this day.

2. And they gave him Aaron, whose sir name was Burr, to go in and out before him, and to stand in his place in certain times; James, whose sir name was Madison, was chief scribe over the people; Henry, whose sir name was Dearbon, was chief in the department of war; Benjamin, whose sir name was Stoddart, was over the ships of war; and Albert, whose sir name was Gallatin, was over the treasury of the people.

3. And Thomas, reigned eight years in Columbia. Moreover he enlarged the borders thereof, greatly, by a purchase from the Emperor of Gaul.

4. Of all that portion of Columbia that lieth west of the great river, called Mississippi, and north of the land called Mexico, and extending unto the great ocean, called Pacific, for the sum of sixty and five score thousand pieces of silver, the same exceeding in extent, all the land taken from the King of Britain, in the war of the Revolution.

5. Now there was war, with the Ishmaelites of the country, called Barbary, in the reign of Thomas the I.

6. For the Rulers of that land, did take the subjects of Columbia, and sell them for slaves.

7. And Thomas sent ships of war to that land, and fought against them, and discomfited them, and from that time; they feared to make slaves, of the men of Columbia.

8. Likewise, was there a conspiracy, to destroy, the goverment in the reign of Thomas; led by Aaron, but by the vigilance of Thomas, it was prevented.

9. Also, was there trouble yet again with the realm of Britian, but the land was not involved in war on account of it, for Thomas, and the men of the Sanhedrim, exercised great wisdom in the matter, insomuch, that peace was maintained.

10. Now the rest of the acts of Thomas, and all that he did, behold, they are written in the book of the records, of the Sanhedrim, at Washington, made during his reign, and the people made James,¶ chief ruler, in his stead, and he commenced to reign.

11. Now James the I, was from the Province of Virginia, and he also, had been one of the mighty ones of the realm. He was moreover excellent in council, and was the agent of Thomas

¶ Madison. 1809.

in the purchase of the country called New France, from the Emperor of Gaul, when Thomas, was Chief Ruler.

12. And they gave him George, whose sir name was Clinton; to go in and out before him, and to stand in his place, in certain times; James, whose sir name was Monroe, was chief scribe over the people; William, whose sir name was Eustis, was chief in the department of war; Paul, whose sir name was Hamilton, was over the ships of war; and Albert, remained over the treasury of the people.

13. Now it came to pass that there was war, in the reign of James, with the realm of Britain; for the men of the ships of the King of Britain, did take the men of the ships of the merchants of Columbia, and compel them to serve, in the ships of the King, of Britain.

14. And when James, and the men of the Sanhedrim, protested unto the King, against this wickedness, Lo! he did justify the acts of his servants, which so enraged the men of Columbia, that they went to war, with the realm of Britain; and this was called the war of Eighteen Hundred and Twelve.

15. And the men of Columbia built swift sailing ships, (the same are called Privateers) and these ships, destroyed of the ships of the merchants of Britain, one score, and three hundred, in the space of three years; also, they took of the ships of the King, not a few.

16. Likewise did the hosts of Columbia, discomfit the hosts of Britain greatly, on the land, insomuch, that they fled to their own land, and after that, they came no more into the land of Columbia, and there was peace once more, between the land of Columbia and the realm of Britain.

17. Also did the Sanhedrim make a law, forbiding the ships of the merchants of Columbia, leaving the ports of the realm, for the space of four score and ten days; and this law, was called an Embargo.

18. Which was the cause of much trouble, and commotion, in the realm, for the business of the merchants was greatly damaged thereby; also did the people, suffer greatly.

19. Likewise, was there war with the Amelakites of the west provinces; but the hosts of Columbia, led by Henry, sir named Harrison, went against them, and fought them at Tip Canoe, and discomfited them, insomuch that they troubled the land no more, at that time.

20. Also, did the Amelakites of the south provinces, make war upon Columbia, and were discomfited, after which they troubled the realm no more, during the reign of James the 1.

21. Likewise, was there again trouble with the Ishmaelites, of Barbary, but they were quickly made to feel the power of Columbia; insomuch that they feared to make war upon her any more, unto this day.

22. Moreover, was the realm increased by the addition of the Province of Louisiana, and Indiana, thereby strengthening her hands greatly.

23. And James reigned eight years in Columbia, and all his acts, and all that he did, behold they are written in

CHAPTER II.

the book of the records of the Sanhedrim, at Washington, made during his reign, and the people made James,‡ the II, chief ruler in his stead, and he commenced to reign.

24. Now James the II, was from the province of Virgina, and he had also been one of the mighty ones of the realm, both in peace, and war, and was much beloved, by the people.

25. And they gave him Daniel, whose sir name was Tompkins, to go in and out before him and to stand in his place, in certain times; John, whose sir name was Adams, was chief scribe over the people; John, whose sir name was Calhoun, was chief in the department of war; Benjamin, whose sir name was Crowningshield, was over the ships of war; and William, whose sir name was Crawford, was over the treasury of the people.

26. Now in the Reign of James the II, did the Amelakites of the south, (the same are called Seminoles) make war upon the realm, but they were quickly put to shame, by the men of Columbia, led by Andrew, and there was peace once more in the land.

27. Likewise were the borders of the realm further increased, by the admission of the provinces of Mississippi and Alabama.

28. Also, was there a treaty of commerce made, with the land called Sweden; and, also, with the realm of Spain.

29. And after that were the borders of the Realm still further enlarged, by the admission of the provinces, of Maine and Missouri.

30. Now the acts of James the II, and all that he did, and the tour that he made of the realm, and the war that he had with the Seminoles, of the south Provinces,

31. Likewise the treaties, that he made with the realms of Britain, and Spain, and the compromise, that was made with the south, in the matter of slavery, (called the Missouri Compromise).

32. Behold they are written in the book of the records, of the Sanhedrim at Washington, made during his reign, and the people made John,§ the II, chief ruler in his stead, and he commenced to reign.

33. Now John the II, was the son of John the I, from the province, of Massachusetts; and like his illustrious father eloquent of tongue; mighty in the Sanhedrim, and firm for liberty.

34. And they gave him John, whose sir name was Calhoun, to go in and out before him, and to stand in his place in certain times; Henry, whose sir name was Clay, was chief scribe over the people; James, whose sir name was Barbour, was chief in the department of war; Samuel, whose sir name was Southard, was over the ships of war; Alexander, whose sir name was McComb, was captain of the host; and Richard, remained over the treasury of the people.

35. And John the II, reigned four years in Columbia, and there was peace all his days, with the nations round about; and the realm did increase greatly in the number of her people

---

‡ Monroe. 1817.

§ Adams. 1825.

36. Albeit, the strife between the Federalists, and Democrats, was exceeding bitter, nevertheless, the land did prosper greatly.

37. Now the acts of John, and all that he did, and the trouble that he had and in money. with the Democratic party, behold they are written in the book of the records, of the Sanhedrim, at Washington, made during his reign; and the people made Andrew, chief ruler in his stead, and he commenced to reign.‖

‖ Jackson. 1829.

NOTE.—The failure to note the appointment of a naval secretary, during the administration of President Washington, might appear to be from neglect, or ignorance, on the part of the writer. But it is neither. No Navy having yet been created, of course no secretary was wanted.

Likewise the small space occupied with the reigns of all the Presidents down to Jackson might seem insufficient, in which, to describe all that occurred, up to that time. But the reader must understand, that these first two Chapters, are merely introductory of what comes after, as the strife for the possession of the government between the whigs and democrats, which commenced with the election of Mr. Jefferson, when the doctrine so disastrous to public and political honesty, was first promulgated, [viz:] that to the victors belong the spoil, [the carrying out of which,' has brought such evil upon the country, by placing in office many incompetent and dishonest men,] had not gained its full strength, until after the reign of Andrew the I, for during his reign, as well as that of Thomas, the democratic party, although in full control of the government, were kept in check. But when the firm hand of Andrew was taken from off the south, and that of the double faced Martin substituted, the flood gates of corruption were thrown wide open, and from that time forth the stream of corruption, incident to, and resultant from the political trickey put in practice, by the leaders of the democratic party in the south, aided by their northern allies, the Dough-faces, continued to increase both in volume and force, until like the Father of Waters at his flood, it o'er flowed the whole land in a rebellion, the like of which for wickedness and cruelty, has never been equalled in any country. The sure handiwork of an unholy lust for power. From Chapter II, to the close, it becomes more full, complete and amusing.

CHAPTER III.

knew, that what-so-ever Andrew said, that would he do!

28. Then did Andrew send ships of war, into the south provinces, unto the city of Charleston, from which city John did come, for it was that city, and province, that did rebel; and he spake thus unto them,

29. Behold, now if ye so much as attempt, to do this thing, as the Lord liveth, I will burn your city with fire, and put you all to the sword, and there shall not a man of you be left alive; verily; you will find it hard to kick against the pricks; Selah.

30. Then did John, and his followers, stay their hand, for they feared Andrew greatly, and there was peace, in the land all the days of Andrew; between the men of the north, and the men of the south.

31. Nevertheless, the hearts of the men of the south, were exceeding bitter against the men of the north.

CHAPTER. IV.

1. Now, there was in those days, in the city of Philadelphia, in the Province of Pensylvania, a certain treasure house called in the venacular, of the realm, the Bank of the Land of Columbia, and it became a snare, unto the people.

2. For the money of the realm was kept therein, and Nicholas, whose sir name was Biddle, (who was over the treasure,) had not only used this money, to corrupt the men of the sanhedrim,

3. But, the people were also made to suffer throughout the realm, from his craftiness, and the power, that the possession of so much money, gave unto him.

4. For when any were to receive money, from this treasure house, then would Nicholas give them paper, when he should give them gold, against the laws of the sanhedrim, as to this matter.

5. And this evil, had become so great, that the wrath of Andrew was kindled, thereat; and he gave command that Nicholas, should come before him.

6. And when he was come into his presence, he spake unto him after this manner;

7. What is this that I hear, that ye not only use the money of the realm, to corrupt the men of the sanhedrim;

8. But, that ye also give the people paper, when ye should give them gold, against the laws regulating the payment of money; behold, this thing that ye do is not good;

9. Now therefore, cease to do this wickedness, any longer, for of a surety, this thing shall not be done, in Columbia.

10. But Nicholas, cared not for the words of Andrew, and he said in the pride of his heart, who is Andrew, that I should regard him; am not I, also one of the mighty ones of this realm,

11. Therefore why should I fear him; or the men of the sanhedrim, for as Sampson did slay his enemies, the Philistines, so will I discomfit mine, yea, and with the self same weapon.

12. Verily, whatsoever seemeth good unto me, to do with the money, that is in my treasure house, that will I do, and no man shall prevent me; and he defied Andrew, and the sanhedrim.

13. Now it came to pass, that the time drew nigh when the people were to elect a chief ruler, (for it was the custom in Columbia to elect every four years) and many of the people were for Andrew, for chief ruler for four years more,

14. And the whole realm was in commotion on account of it; but the friends of Nicholas, were exceeding zealous against Andrew.

15. And Andrew wrote a proclamation, and sent it out among the people, in the which he certified them, that if he became chief ruler, for four years more, that then, would he destroy the treasure house, of Nicholas, in the city of Philadelphia.

16. Then were the people glad; when they saw the writing of the proclamation, for they said of a certainty, is this thing too mighty for us.

17. Now, therefore let us make Andrew chief ruler for four years more, and then shall Nicholas, be destroyed, for verily, whatsoever Andrew saith, that will he do; and thus shall this great evil be removed, from the realm.

18. And the people made Andrew, chief ruler, for four years more; and he took the money out of the house of Nicholas, and put it in certain places called, sub-treasurys; and he destroyed the house of Nicholas, in the city of Philadelphia,

19. And when the men of the sanhedrim, saw what Andrew had done they were filled with rage, and they said unto him,

20. Why have ye done this, behold ye have caused the gains, that we did get from Nicholas, to cease, to our great damage.

21. Then was Andrew wroth, and he said unto them, did I not certainly say unto you, that if I became chief ruler, the second time, that I would destroy the house of Nicholas, that is in the city of Philadelphia.

22. And that I would take the money, of the realm therefrom, and have I not done it; therefore why say ye unto me, why do ye so.

23. Verily, the money of the realm shall not remain in the house of Nicholas; but in the treasure house that I have prepared for it, have I not said it;

24. Of a certainty, Nicholas shall lend the money of the realm, unto you no more forever; selah.

25. And it came to pass, that this thing made great commotion, in the land, but Andrew was firm; and thus was this great evil removed from the realm.

26. Likewise, was there trouble with the realm of Gaul, in the reign of Andrew, for the King of Gaul, thought to go to war with Columbia, but the wisdom, and firmness of Andrew, together with the men of the sanhedrim, did prevent it.

27. And Andrew, reigned eight years in Columbia, and all his acts, and all that he did, and the war that he had with the Seminoles of the south provinces,

28. Also, the war that he had, with the Amelekites of the west provinces; (called the Black Hawk war,) and the tour that he made of the north provinces,

29. Behold, they are written in the book of the records, of the sanhedrim at Washington made during his reign, and the people made Martin, chief ruler, in his stead, and he commenced to reign.*

---

*1837. Van Buren.

CHAPTER. V.

1. Now all these men, that had been chief rulers of Columbia, down to the reign of Martin the I, were mighty men; men of renown, yea; they were mighty, in word, and deed; and it was by their wisdom in council, firmness in the sanhedrim, and courage in war, that the land was freed from the King of Britain, and exalted among the nations.

2. Moreover, the laws that they made, were for the best good of all the people; and the realm had prospered exceedingly, insomuch, that the whole earth, stood in fear of its power.

3. Yea; if a man in any other land, should say unto the rulers thereof; I am a citizen of Columbia, then would those rulers fear to harm him, for of a certainty, would Columbia defend him.

4. But now, alas for Columbia, the mighty men that founded the government, and who had also been her first chief rulers, were passing away, some of them already slept with their fathers; and a new generation, and in part, a new race; were to rule the land.

6. Men that were incompetent, men of small ability as chief rulers, men that were dishonest, men that sought their own exaltation, and not the best good of the realm, and of which, Martin, was the true exponent.

7. For verily, (with two exception,) the chief rulers of Columbia, from the reign of Andrew the I, unto the reign of Abraham the I, were not mighty men, neither were they men of renown, but like Absalom, the son of David; they sought their own agrandizement, and not the best good of the realm.

8. And they did, one and all, do all that they could, to strengthen the slave power, and destroy liberty, until the land was filled with violence, and anarchy had begun to prevail, neither did they stay their hand; until they had plunged the nation in a civil war, in the reign of Abraham the I.

9. Also, was the Sanhedrim filled with men, that were not like the men of the days of George, and John the I, for with few exceptions, they were men of no ability as councelors, their wisdom was foolishness, and they did the realm much damage.

10. For many of them drank strong waters, and took bribes, and practiced simony, and did many exceeding wicked and foolish things, insomuch that the government had become contempable, for its wickedness and folly.

11. Also, many of them were the degenerated sons of men that were loyalists, when the land was a province of the realm of Britain, and Tories, when the people were fighting for their liberties against the king, but in the reign of Thomas, they began to be called democrats.

CHAPTER III.

1. Now Andrew the I, was a mighty man of war, had been long in the land, was much beloved by the people; was from the Province of Tennessee, and of the Democratic party, for that party, was then in power, in the Land.

2. And they gave him John, whose sir name was Calhoun, to go in and out before him, and to stand in his place, in certain times; Martin, whose sir name was VanBuren, was chief scribe over the people; John, whose sir name was Eaton, was chief in the department of war; John, whose sir name was Branch, was over the ships of war; Winfield, was captain of the host; and Samuel, whose sir name was Ingham, was over the treasury of the people.

3. Now there was at this time in the south provinces, certain men and women, that had black skins, and they were held by the people of those provinces, as slaves; and this thing had become a curse! unto the whole realm.

4. And this evil, had existed in the land since the time when it was a province of the realm of Britain.

5. For the merchants of the realm of Britain, that sent ships to a country called Africa, that lieth to the eastward of the ocean called Atlantic, did steal the inhabitants of that land, and sell them, to the people of Columbia, for slaves.

6. And they had multiplied exceedingly, and filled the land, insomuch that when George, was made the first chief ruler, they were in every province, even thirteen, for that was the number at that time; but when Andrew the I, became chief ruler, the number of provinces was twenty and three; and these people, were sold in the markets, like the beasts of the field.

7. Now George the I, had great wisdom, even like Solomon of old, and he foresaw, that this thing would prove a snare, and a curse; in years to come; and in an epistle, that he left unto the people, (called a farewell address) he warned them to cast it out of the land.

8. And the people of the north provinces cast it out; but the people of the south provinces, did retain it.

9. For they said behold, this thing is good for us, likewise is it good for the black man; also, yea, for this end was he made, and we will not let him go free; but he shall be our bondsman, and his seed after him, forever, and no man shall prevent it.

10. Now this thing had made some disturbance in the reign of James the II, for when the north had cast it out, then did the men of the south say unto them

11. Give ye us now a pledge, that ye will not molest slavery, in the south provinces, for we are fearful that ye will deal deceitfully with us, in this matter, in years to come.

12. This do, and all shall be well, but if ye do not this, then will we destroy this confederacy, (for the government was called a confederation of states) and form a new one,—

13. In which slavery, shall be the chief corner stone, for verily, this matter of slavery, that ye make so much noise about, we will not surrender.

14. For notwithstanding, that the men of the south, had in former times, made an agreement, with the men of the north, called the ordinance of seventeen hundred and eighty-seven,

15. In the which, all north of a certain line (called Mason and Dixon's line,) was to be free; and all south of that line, for slavery, yet did they demand this additional agreement.

16. Albeit, it was not in their thoughts, to abide by either of these agreements, being fully determined, that slavery, should again extend throughout the realm.

17. For it came to pass, after Andrew, became chief ruler, that John, called Calhoun, together with others, that were chiefs of the south provinces, entered into a conspiracy, to destroy the government of Columbia.

18. And John, became their leader, and he spake unto Andrew, and the men of the Sanhedrim, after this manner.

19. "Give ye us now more pledges —in the matter of Slavery; or we will destroy this government, for we are determined to rule this land, and ye cannot prevent it."

20. But the men of the north said; "stand to the agreement that you have made with us, and ye shall suffer no harm;" but John said, "nay, we will not stand to our agreement,

21. Therefore give ye us now the pledges, that we shall ask, or my province will rebel, for we are determined to do this thing, if we get not the pledges;

22. And they said unto John, "behold, we have already ma'e two agreements with you, touching this matter, and ye refuse to abide by them,"

23. What surety then have we, that ye will abide by a new one, verily ye are asking an unreasonable thing, of us, and we shall make no new agreement with you, touching this matter.

24. But John answered the men of the north, after this manner; "behold ye cannot trifle with us, for we are as one man, and if ye give us not the pledges; then shall ye surely have war."

25. Then was the wrath of Andrew kindled against John, and his countenance was changed; and he said unto his servants, behold, now what these Rebels, would do unto us.

26. Now, therefore, as the Lord liveth, and I live, if John, whose sir name is Calhoun, be found in this city to-morrow, after the sun be risen, I will hang him fifty cubits high, Selah!

27. And it came to pass, when John was told, the words of Andrew, that great fear came upon him, and he fled, to a place of safety, until the wrath of Andrew should abate, for he well

CHAPTER V.

12. Now it came to pass, after the people had become free, that they made a law, and this was the meaning of the law, that no man, whether he be born in the realm, or if he come from the realms of the Kings across the water, should be an elector (the same meaneth a voter), if he had not dwelt in the land, one score and one years.

13. For they said, how can a man be an elector, if he be ignorant of the laws, or how can he understand the laws, if he be not born in the realm, unless he remain in it, until he shall know them.

14. Moreover, are not many of the people that come from other lands, unlearned in this matter, having never been electors, in their own land.

15. How then shall they be preferred before one born in the realm, nay, verily let them dwell therein until they become instructed in this matter; and understand the laws, before they become electors.

16. For doth not the child creep, before it can walk, how much more then, should a man learn to be ruled, before he be a ruler.

17. Now the party in favor of this law, were called Whigs, which meaneth, true men, and liberty; and the party that did oppose it, were called Democrats, which meaneth, lovers of strong waters, and slavery.

18. Albeit, there were many of that party, that were true men; nevertheless it was the slave-holders party.

19. And this party had been getting stronger, and stronger, in the land since the reign of Thomas the I, and they were in favor of changing the law, in the matter of electors.

20. For they said if we do this, then will the men of other lands join themselves unto us, and by their help, will we get control of the government, and the strife between these two parties was exceeding bitter.

21. Now of those that had come from the realms across the water, many had already joined themselves unto that party, for they said; this is the party that will make of us electors, yea, and rulers, and they clave unto them.

22. Albeit, those that came from that part of the realm of Britain, that is called Albion, did most join themselves unto the Whigs, for they were for liberty.

CHAPTER VI.

1. Now Albion, is an exceeding old and powerful realm, neither is there any like unto her, or that can excel her, in the wealth, and pride, of her nobles, or her merchants, and in the glory of her conquests, there is none that approacheth unto her, except the ancient realms, of Hispania, and Gaul.

2. And these three old nations have been the Pioneers, in the discovery of new worlds, and it was by the aid of Spain, that Columbus, was enabled to make the voyage, in the which he discovered Columbia.

3. Whereupon, that nation planted her colonies in the southern portion thereof, and for many long years, did her subjects desolate the land with fire, and sword, in their insane thirst for gold.

4. While the men of Gaul, entering by the great river of Canada; claimed and occupied, all the northern portion thereof, in which they got exceeding much wealth, from the Amelakites; and the Jebusites, that occupied the land.

5. Now the cupidity of the men of Albion, caused them to not only desire the possession of that portion of Columbia, that is called New England, in which the Pilgrim Fathers had already found a home, but they desired the possession of the whole realm, also.

6. Therefore, did they make war, upon the men of Hispania and Gaul, for its posession, neither did they stay their hand, until they had wrested it from them, and Columbia became a province of Albion, until the war of the Revolution.

7. Albeit, that part which lieth west of the great river called Mississippi came not into the possession of Albion, but remained as a province of Gaul, until purchased (as before stated) by Columbia, when Thomas was chief ruler.

8. Likewise, did Hispania retain that portion called Florida, until after Columbia had become free; when it also; by treaty, and purchase, became a part of the realm.

9. But in the war of the Revolution, was the pride of old Albion greatly humbled, and her power broken, insomuch, that she was compelled to let the people of Columbia, go out free.

10. For in the pride of their hearts, had the King, and Lords of Albion thought to enslave the men of Columbia, and do unto them, as did Pharao of old, unto the children of Israel.

11. But the God of Battles sent them a Leader, in the person of George the first chief ruler, who delivered them out of bondage, and put the King, and his Lords to shame.

12. Now not only was the rule or

CHAPTER VI.

Albion's ancient Kings and Lords very severe over all her subjects;

13. But over the men that composed her armies, was it exceedingly so; insomuch that it was grevious to bear.

14. Which caused them, when they had seen Columbia; that it was a goodly land, and fair; to greatly desire to be numbered among its inhabitants: and escape from their bondage, as had the Pilgrim Fathers, long years before.

15. Therefore was it, that when compelled by their rulers, to fight against their bretheren, and the sacred cause of Liberty, that many of them did desert, the King, and join themselves unto the men of Columbia.

16. And thus was the cause of liberty strengthened, somewhat, by those that its enemies had sent to destroy it.

17. Nevertheless, no realm on the globe, is to-day, so grand and powerful, as is Albion, except Columbia, and to her; belongeth the highest place among the nations.

18. Grand indeed is Columbia, the joy of the earth, the pride of the nations, the home of the oppressed, and to this high place, hath she been exalted, by the power of her free public schools.

19. While Hispania, once so warlike, and proud, and whose fleets of treasure ships, once covered the seas, the envied of the nations.

20. To-day lies buried in the grave of bigotry, and superstition, prepared for her by the Romish Church, and out of which, it doth not appear that for her, there can be any resurection, forever.

21. For upon her hath the church of Rome, done its perfect will, and through her, are all its beauties, made visible, unto the nations.

22. Alas, for thee Hispania, the proud, the land of Torquemada, and Loyola, the Inquisition, and the Fagot, how art thou fallen, from thy high place.

23. Thy sunny soil, is strewn; with human wrecks, thy people, in mental chains, and thy very name; hath become a stench, in the nostrils, of the nations.

24. Moreover, whatsoever, thou touchest is accursed, for thy hands are red, with human slaughter; and thou hast, done more wickedness, in the name of religion, than any other nation, upon the Earth.

25. And for this cause, hast thou fallen, from thy position, as one of the grandest of the old nations, until thou hast become, the most contemptable.

26. Sad, indeed, is thy condition. Thy Kings in Exile; thy government, in the hands, of an unscrupulous and corrupt Priesthood, with no star of hope, to lead thee, on to freedom, and fame, for there are no free schools, in thy borders.

27. But, in stead thereof, hath one long, endless night of superstition, closed over thee, and, except ye shall break, the Romish Yoke, you are lost forever.

28. And France, La Belle France, the ancient realm of Gaul, whose fierce warriors, so valliantly withstood the legions of Old Roma, two thousand years ago,

29. And whose armies, under the great Napoleon, became the terror of

the nations, in more modern times, with a history, so full, of glorious memories.

30. Lies bleeding, also, and helpless, at the feet of her ancient and inveterate foe, in consequence, of the corrupting, and blighting influences, of this same, great enemy, of all human liberty and progress.

NOTE.—The German-Franco War of 1870, fully illustrates the truths contained in this Chapter. Both Germany and France, are old, as well as powerful Nations,—both were at one time, wholly Catholic; *even their kings*, were named by the Pope, yet, look at the result, of this contest. —The minions of Bigotry and Despotism, were sadly beaten, and put to shame. And the cause for it, is to be found in this. Germany (thanks to Martin Luther,) has shaken off her fetters, and come out, into the light, and by her system of education, each of her subjects, is made to feel that he is a part, of the great whole. While France, upon whose dominions, as upon those of England, it might with truth be said, that the Sun never sets.—Has, by remaining wholly under the control of the Church of Rome; lost her ancient self-respect, and manhood.—Her kingly race, have run to waste, having spent their time, and talents, upon that which corrupts, both body, and mind. And in consequence of this, instead of her armies, driving all Europe before them, as in former times.—In this contest, they won not one battle, but were compelled to see their beloved France, in the posession, of the grand old Kaiser William, and his army.—What a change from her former days. In Germany, all can read, but in France, it is not so, neither will it be, until she too steps out into the light, establishes a system of free schools, and religious toleration Then, *and not until then*, will she regain the power, that she had under the great Napoleon. Verily, what is wanted in France, is a Bismark!

CHAPTER VII.

1. Now in the western portion of Albion's Isle, lieth a mountainous region, called Wales, and it is also a part of the realm of Britain.

2. And its people were in ancient times called Siluers: the most fierce and warlike, of all the tribes that belonged to the ancient realm of Albion.

3. And Albion's ancient kings, had more trouble to subdue them, than any other of the numerous tribes, that today acknowledge her sway.

4. For they defended themselves with great skill, and courage, for many years, until finally (more by compromise, than conquest,) they became incorporated into, and made a part of that realm, in the reign of Edward the I.

5. Now these people are hardy, industrious, and very intelligent, but of a quick, and hasty temper; possessed of much national pride, and can boast a long line of noble ancestry.

6. For they are an ancient race; speaking a language, the like whereof hath no other people, except the Gaels, or Celts, neither can it be certainly known from whence they sprung.

7. Moreover, are they a nation of miners, more so than are the men of Albion, except that part called Cornwall, for Wales, is full of the precious metals.

8. Likewise are they exceeding skilful, in the working of iron, and steel, in which they excel, and in their love of country, no race of men can surpass them.

9. And to this land came the ships of Ancient Tyre, and Carthage, three thousand years ago, for tin and iron.

10. Also, are they fond of music, and in olden time, their Bards were noted for their skill upon the harp.

11. And many of these men came also, to Columbia, and joined themselves, unto the party called whigs.

12. Now these people are a benefit, to any land, for they are a God fearing and a law abiding race, full of courage, firm for liberty, and mostly of the faith called Protestant.

13. Happy is any land, whose people are as intelligent, industrious and God fearing as are the men, of Wales; for then, will that land surely prosper.

CHAPTER. VIII.

1. Likewise, is there a land to the north of ancient Albion; also a part of the present realm of Britain, that was in ancient times, called Caledonia, but is known at this day, as Scotland; and many of her sons came to Columbia.

2. Now Scotland is a beautiful land wherein to dwell, abounding in fertile vales, that are lovely to the eye, also hath it great mountains, whose hoary heads are crowned with the blue-bell, and the heather, and whose massive feet, are bathed in "Lochs," the like whereof, can no other land excel in beauty.

3. And its ancient inhabitants, were called Gaels, or Picts; a bold and warlike race, even more so than were the men of Albion, with whom they were constantly at war, until by compromise, (more than by conquest,) their country, became a part of that Realm.

4. Yea, so fierce and bold were these ancient Gaels, that the Emperor, of Roma, was compelled to build a wall, upon the northern border of Albion, to prevent them from devastating, that isle, when it was a Roman province; that is known as Adrian's Wall, unto this day.

5. Now the men of Scotland, are a strong, and hardy race, fond of manly sports, and of their ancient music, the pipes, the like of which, hath no other **nation,** and the music of which, in ancient times, so fired their martial spirit, as to cause them to assault their foes; with a fury, that nothing could withstand.

6. Also, were they in ancient times, divided into Clans, under hereditary chiefs, to both of which, they were loyal, and true.

7. Proud, and haughty, were these ancient Highland chiefs, submitting to no authority, but their own will, making constant forays, upon each other, and upon Albion, until finally, incorporated into, and made a part of that realm.

8. Since which time, they have been loyal and true, in their allegience to her, shedding their blood for her defence and honor, in all her wars, unto this day.

9. Neither hath she any subjects, upon whom she hath confered greater honors, or who are more worthy, than are the men of Caledonia.

10. Likewise do they yield perfect obedience unto the laws, of any land, wherein they come, therefore do the rulers, like much, to have them for subjects.

11. For they are both intelligent, and learned, and are well qualified, for electors, and rulers, also, are they very shrewd, at money getting, and in the management, of the financial offices of the realm, have they no su-

I BOOK CHRONICLES,

perior.

12. Also, are many of them skilled in astronomy, geology, medicine, and the mechanical arts; and for many of the most important discoveries, of modern times, are we indebted, to the men of Caledonia.

13. Likewise have many of them been great explorers, in other lands, and written many books thereon, for the benefit of the people.

14. Many of them also, are skilled in the building of ships, also do they excel, in the working of iron and steel, and in the manufacture of cotton, and woolen goods.

15. But, in their love for the faith, called Protestant, are they grand; neither can any nation, excel them, in their boldness, or zeal, in its defence.

16. Yea, so firmly was that faith, instilled into the men of Caledonia, in the days of John Knox, that all the craft, and power of the church of Rome, has been powerless, to destroy it.

17. Neither can it be destroyed, for they are temperate, and orderly, in all that they do; their children also, do they bring up, in the fear of God, and Him do they acknowledge, in all their ways.

18. Also are they satisfied with the civil, and religious liberty, that they enjoy, in this land, neither do they seek, to change the laws, made in the days, of the first chief rulers, in the matter of electors, or to destroy the liberties, of the people.

19. Therefore do the people exalt them, to places of trust, because they are worthy, for of a certainty, Columbia hath no better men, in all her borders, than are the men of Caledonia.

CHAPTER IX.

1. Now there lieth to the east of the realm of Britain, and Gaul, a land called Germany, the same in ancient times was called Germania.

2. Now Germany is a large and fair land, yea exceeding fair, moreover its hills are clothed with the vines, from which its people do make the wine; that so rejoiceth the heart of man.

3. And the inhabitants of that land, were in ancient times called Teutones, which meaneth ancient men, for they claim, to be the oldest of the nations.

4. Also, were they in ancient times an exceeding fierce, and warlike people, insomuch, that the armies of old Roma, had much trouble, to subdue them.

5. Now this people, had long been ruled by kings, and emperors, with great severity, therefore was it, that when told Columbia, was a free land, that they desired greatly, to become its subjects.

6. And they said one to the other, why tarry we here, in this land of tyranny and oppression, verily, if we escape not hence, we shall all be destroyed.

7. Therefore, let us arise, and take our wives, and our little ones, and our goods, also our money, and go to the land of Columbia, and join ourselves, unto the inhabitants of that land.

8. For behold that is a free land, and exceeding fair, there, can we get us homes, for ourselves, our wives, and our little ones, which we cannot do here.

9. For of a surety, much gold, will not purchase for us homes, in this land, but in Columbia, it is not so.

10. Then, did these people arise, and take their wives, and their little ones, and their money, and gat them to Columbia, until it was full of them.

11. Yea, from one extremity of the land, unto the other, they were in numbers, like the leaves of the forest.

12. Now these people are a strong, and lasty race, fond of money-getting, very intelligent, (for they can all read,) good to work, being compelled by their rulers, to labor diligently in their own land; and in religious faith, are they both Catholics, and Protestant.

13. Likewise, are they very skillful, in the working of all kinds of metal, gold, silver, iron, and brass; also all manner of precious stones, and in music; they excel every other nation.

14. Now it is the law, of Germany, that every child, shall be instructed, so that it can read, and if the parents neglect to do this, then will the rulers, compel them, therefore can they all read.

15. Also, shall they learn some art,

so that they be a help, and not a burden, unto any land, wherein they dwell.

16. Moreover, are some of them exceeding learned, in the arts, and sciences, chemistry, philosophy, astronomy, and geology, many of them being men of great intellect, also do they write many books.

17. Now, these people are much given to pleasure, also to the use of the filthy weed, called tobacco; that groweth in Columbia. Yea, so filthy is this vile weed, that no one of the brute creation, will eat of it, except, the unclean goat.

18. Likewise, have they great buildings, the same are called breweries, in which they make the drink, called Lager Beer, for themselves, also do they sell, unto the people of the realm, and get exceeding, much gain thereby.

19. Nevertheless, they are diligent in business, both in the city, and in the plain, and make the land to blossom like the rose, for they are exceeding skilful, in the working of the soil, and in the cultivation of flowers, do they excel.

20. Likewise do they delight in military pomp, and show; and in war they are good soldiers, and Columbia, hath no better men, in her armies, than are the men of Germany.

21. Now these people, are exceeding tenacious of their liberties, like much to be made electors, and rulers, insomuch, that the realm, hath been greatly damaged, thereby.

22. For many of them became rulers, that are unworthy; the evil of which, Columbia, doth suffer from, unto this day.

23. For the Democratic party, made of these men, electors, and rulers, before they could speak the language, of the realm, much less did they understand its laws; or the customs of its people.

24. Albeit; there were some that would not do this great folly, and they joined themselves unto the Whigs, being firm for liberty.

CHAPTER. X.

1. Now to the north of Germany, and east of Albion, there lieth a land, that in ancient times was called Scandinavia; but at this day, it is known as Denmark, Norway, and Sweden.

2. And the inhabitants of these three realms, are an exceeding robust, and hardy race, all of the faith called Protestant, or Lutheran, and many of them, came also to Columbia.

3. Now the men of Norway, (who were the ancient Sitones,) are exceeding fond of the sea, and their wise men claim, that they discovered Columbia, eight hundred years ago, and planted a colony therein, in the province of Massachusetts, which they called Vineland, on account, of the great quantity of wild grapes, found at that place.

4. Also were they in ancient times, called Sea Rovers, which meaneth, men that discover new countries and conquer them.

5. Neither is there any that can excel them, in boldness, or endurance, for they are strong, hardy, and patient, and the ships of Columbia, are full of them.

6. Also are they fond of tilling the soil, some of the north provinces, being full of them, and in this, also, are they greatly prospered, and the realm benefited thereby.

7. For they are both industrious, and frugal, neither do they seek to be made rulers, before they understand the laws of the realm, (as do many of the Germans,) whereby the cause of true liberty, is greatly damaged.

8. Likewise are the men of Denmark, and Sweden, among the best of Columbia's foriegn born citizens, for they are a God fearing people, obedient unto the laws, temperate, and orderly, in all that they do.

9. Now the men of Denmark, were in ancient times, called Cimbri, and were one of the most fierce, and warlike, of all the ancient tribes, of Scandinavia.

10. Making war continually, upon all the nations round about them, being at one time, the rulers of proud, and haughty Albion, yea, some of the grandest of her time honored ruins, were built, in the days, of her Danish rulers.

11. Also, did both they, and the men of Norway, make forays into the ancient realms, of Hispania, and Gaul, two thousand years ago, devastating them both, with fire, and sword, for many long years.

12. Fierce, and bold, were those ancient warriors, of old Scandinavia, with an aspect terrible to behold, putting to shame, and driving before them, (as the herdsman driveth his flock,) three of the armies of old Roma, in succession, and passing the mighty Alps, they threatened the seven hilled city itself.

CHAPTER X.

13. But the fourth was sent against them, led by the renowned Caius Marius, by which they were put to flight, and Rome, saved, for that time, from destruction, by these northern vandals.

14. But these men of Scandinavia, that come to our shores, are not so, moreover, do they bring much gold, and silver, wherewith to buy for themselves homes; and the treasury of the realm, hath been greatly enriched thereby.

15. And they joined themselves, unto the party, called Whigs, being all true men, and firm for liberty.

16. Better would it be for Columbia, if all that come to her shores, from the realms across the water, were as temperate, orderly, and God fearing, as are the men of Caledonia, and Scandinavia, for then, would, Columbia, be the delight of the nations.

17. But alas for her, this is not so, and unless this lust for power, and money, that is burning in the hearts of the people, be quenched;

18. Then, is the time, not far distant, that will behold her, humbled in the dust, for a certainty, will God judge her, for her sins.

CHAPTER XI.

1. Now to the west of Albion, lieth a land, that in ancient times, was called Hibernia; but at this day, it is called Ireland, and is a part, of the realm of Britain.

2. Also, is it called the Emerald Isle, likewise the Gem of the Sea, on account of its exceeding great beauty.

3. For it is a beautiful land, fair to look upon; yea, it aboundeth in hills, and vales, that are lovely, to the eye, also, hath it great rivers, and is moreover surrounded by the sea.

4. Now, in this land, there are no poisonous reptiles, neither are there any snakes, or serpents, neither toads, or frogs, for Saint Patrick, (the patron Saint of that land,) banished them all from its soil.

5. And it was the abode of the *Connaught-ite*, the *Munster-ite*, the *Galway-ite*, the *Tipperary-ite*, the *Limerick-ite*, the *Corck-ite*, the *Killarney-ite*, the Men of Meath, The White Boys, the Short Boys, the Fardowners; and all these people, and tribes, were of the race called Celts, and were in numbers, like the sands of the sea.

6. Now, they had dwelt there for long ages past, under their own kings, but at length they gat at war, among themselves, (for they were a restless, and turbulent race,) and thereby brought ruin, and destruction, upon their own heads.

7. For the King, of the Realm of Britain, near whose dominions their country did lie, took this opportunity to make war upon them, and subdue them; and they have been subject unto that Realm, unto this day.

8. Now the wars, they had among themselves, had impoverished them greatly, but the King of Britain, stripped them, of all their worldly possessions, that were left, and they were in great want.

9. And he gave their lands, unto his lords, and mighty men, and they became the serfs, or tenants, of these lords, and worked the land, for their benefit.

10. Also, did the King appoint governors over them, that were not of their race; and he also compelled them, to give the one-tenth part, of all that they had, for the support of the Image, that he had set up in his dominions, called the Established Church.

11. And he also made a Decree, that no man, of that land, should be a ruler, unless he would worship the Image, that he had set up.

12. Now these people were of the faith, that is called Roman Catholic, and they were moreover, firmly fixed in that faith, neither would they abjure it.

13. Therefore were they persecuted and oppressed, by the King, and peo-

CHAPTER XI.

ple of Britain, until they became of all men, the most miserable.

14. For between the King and people on one side, and the rule of their Priests, on the other side, they were in a great strait.

15. For the Bishops, and Priests, of the Romish Church, kept them in a worse state of slavery, (mentally) than did their civil Rulers, their bodies; so that between the two, they were in a hard place.

16. Yea, the Iron-Heel of the Church of Rome, is on the necks, of this down-trodden people, unto this day, to the great damage of themselves, and of any land, wherein they may dwell.

17. For they are kept in ignorance of many things, that are for their best good, by this corrupt Church, neither can they escape, from the bondage, in which they are held, by these ecclesiastical task-masters.

18. Yea, this Church, is to-day, at war, against the free schools of Columbia, in which our children, are taught those things, that make them good citizens, and are determined to destroy them, and to cut down the tree of liberty, that was planted by our Fathers.

19. Now, most of these people, possessed neither houses, or lands; but they dwelt in huts, and for food, they had potatoes and salt, and often, they had not these.

20. For there came a time, when the land was smitten with sickness, and their crops did rot, before the time for the harvest had came, and the land was bare.

21. Therefore were they in great distress, and want; yet would not their cruel task-masters, lighten their burdens, but did still demand their rents. for the soil.

22. Now these exactions, and oppressions, together with the famine in the land, did at last so reduce, this miserable, and unfortunate people, that great numbers of them died of starvation, and Ireland, became a vast poor house.

23. And Columbia, sent ships, filled with food, to the starving men and women of that unfortunate land, the gift of a generous Nation.

24. Now these people are a strong, and hardy race, of a generous disposition, quick to resent an insult, good to work, (and for children,) no nation on earth, can excel them, in the number thereof.

25. Also, are they exceeding witty, full of mirth, fond of all kind of amusement, and were it not for the yoke put upon their necks, by the Church of Rome, no people on the earth, would excel them, in all that makes a nation great.

26. Now, great numbers of their children, grow up in ignorance, and vice, for the Priests, will not suffer them, to go to the free schools, (if they can prevent it,) to the great damage of the Realm.

27. Likewise are they exceeding fond of strong waters, many of them being continually filled therewith, and this also, is the cause of much trouble, to themselves, and their Rulers.

28. And this poison, was called

"Potheen," in their own land; but in Columbia, it is called whisky, which meaneth, the broth of hell.

29. Now it was the law, of the Realm of Britain, that if any would drink this vile stuff, that then, should they pay a tax, therefor, into the Treasury of the King, whether it was made in the Realm, or came from foreign parts.

30. And the King appointed certain, officers, (the same are called Gaugers,) to collect this tax, and the whole land, was filled with violence, in consequence thereof.

31. For the men of Ireland, not only refused to obey this law, but they also worried the servants of the King, not a little, yea, they often took their lives, and the King, could not enforce, his decree in that land.

32. But the people still continued to make this "Potheen," in secret, for themselves, also, did they sell unto their brethern, in bondage, to the great damage, not only of themselves, but also to the Treasury of the King.

CHAPTER XII.

1. And it came to pass, when the King of the Realm of Britain, saw that he could not enforce his decree, in regard to Strong Waters, in the land called Ireland,

2. —That he was exceeding wroth, and his countenance was changed, and he sent for his counsellors, and his wise men, and when they were come before him, he spake unto them, after this manner.

3. Lo, these men of the faith, called Roman Catholic, in Ireland, do make exceeding much commotion, and disturbance in the Realm.

4. Verily, they are a lawless, and turbulent race, and there is no good in them, neither, can their like be found, in any nation.

5. For behold, they do utterly refuse, to obey the law of the Realm, in the matter of the tax, upon Strong Waters, and have set at defiance my authority, neither, will they worship, the Image, that I have set up.

6. Likewise, have they stoned my servants, that were sent unto them, to receive that, which was mine own; and some of them, have they basely slain.

7. Now therefore, what shall be done, with these rebels, for they regard no mans authority; but are wholly under the control, of their Priests, verily, is the whole Realm, in a constant turmoil, on account of them, neither, can it have any rest, until they be sent out of it.

8. And they answered the King, after this manner, the thing that the King, purposeth, to do, is good, therefore let it be done, and then, shall the Realm, be rid of these turbulent, and lawless people.

9. Then, said the King, yea, but whereunto, shall we send them, for of a certainty, is there no Realm, this side the great waters, that will receive them, and when the King, knew not what to do, one of the Council, spoke thus unto the King,

10. Behold; there is the Land of Columbia, peradventure, the rulers of that land will receive them, for that is a large land, and free, neither, is there any tax upon Strong Waters, in Columbia.

11. And this Council, pleased the King, and he sent them to Columbia, until it was full of them, in the city, and in the plain, they were like grasshoppers, for multitude.

12. Now when the men of Columbia, (that were of the whig party,) saw these people, it came to pass that they were filled with astonishment, and they said one to the other.

13. Behold, ye see what the King of Britain, hath done unto us, verily he is filling Columbia, with paupers.

14. Were it not enough, that the men of Germany, have well nigh taken the land, and thereby put the government, into the hands of our enemies, the democrats; surely, we would that this cup might pass from us.

15. Albeit, these Germans do bring much gold, into the Realm, also are they very intelligent, and will in no wise, become a burden, unto the land of their adoption.

(16. For as before stated, not only had many of the men called Hessians, that the King of Britain, had sent over in the war of the Revolution, settled in the land—

17. But the province of New York, and likewise that of Pennsylvania, were mostly filled with the men or Germany, that came as emigrants, both before, and after the war.

18. A sufficient number of which had joined the Whig party, to enable that party, to keep possession of the government, until the Reign of Thomas the I, at which time the Democratic party, first begun to be strong, in Columbia.)

19. But these men of Ireland, that the King of Britain, hath sent unto Columbia, are not so.

20. And surely, unless they can be released, from the bondage of the Romish Church, and instructed, they will prove both a burden, and a curse.

21. Therefore let us set them at work, and also instruct them, in all the things that are necessary, for them to know, in order to become good citizens, for of a certainty have they had small chance, in their own land.

22. Now there were in Columbia, at this time, many mighty works being done, for the people were making great rivers, the same are called canals, also great highways, called Rail Roads, and these people, did they cause to labor, upon these works.

23. For they were strong, and willing, also do they delight exceedingly to delve in the earth, yea, more so than do the men, of any other nation.

24. But, when the leaders of the Democratic party, beheld them, and saw that they were strong, and willing to work; it came to pass, that they rejoiced greatly, and said one to the other, behold, these are they, that shall help us into power.

25. For although they have eyes, yet they see not, ears, yet they hear not; neither do they understand, what is for their own good.

26. Surely, did we have much trouble, to bring the men of Germany, over unto us, for they are a very cautious people, and hard to deceive, (for they can all read.)

27. But these men of Ireland, are not so; verily the wild ass, of the desert, is not more stupid, than are they, in matters of government, or in what is for their own good, for thanks to the Romish Church, (few of them can read.)

28. Therefore shall they not see the snares, that we shall put in their way, and we shall lead them captive, at our will.

29. Surely, is the hand of the Lord, in this, and we will yet possess, this land, and get exceeding much treasure, for hath it not been the watchword of our party, since the reign of Thomas

CHAPTER XII.

the 1. that to the victors, belong the spoil.

30. Therefore, shall the Whig, be unto us, as a hired servant, neither shall his purse, from this time forth, contain any scrip;—selah.

31. And they spake softly, unto them, saying, come ye over unto us, for the people have spoken good, concerning us.

32. Surely, ye are like unto us, in that ye love Strong Waters, moreover, it, and Slavery, are the rocks, upon which our party is built.

33. Therefore, join yourselves unto us, and ye shall not only become electors, but ye shall also be made rulers, likewise, shall ye be filled with Strong Waters, continually—

34. Neither shall ye pay any thing, into the treasury of the Realm, therefor, as ye were compelled to do in your own land, for thanks to us, this vile stuff is free, in Columbia.

35. Now it came to pass, when they heard the words, of these traitors, against the liberties of the people, that they rejoiced greatly, for verily, no race of men, upon the whole earth, do love office, or to be made rulers, as do the men of Ireland.

36. And they joined themselves, unto the Democratic party, in such numbers, that when Andrew the I, was made chief ruler, that party, had, by their help, got possession of the government.

37. For they had changed the laws, made in the days, of George, and John the I, so that if a man be in Columbia, for the space of three years, that then, could he be an elector, yea, and a ruler.

38. By which change the Democratic party, joined hands, with the Church of Rome, hoping thereby, to possess the land, for themselves, and to perpetuate their rule therein.

39. While the Church, seeks to use that party, as the weapon, wherewith to destroy the Tree of Liberty, and to plant that of Bigotry, and Superstition, in its stead.

40. (For of a certainty, whomsoever, the Democratic party, seek to make chief ruler, for that man, will the Romish Church, cast her vote.)

41. Thus was Columbia the fair, like Sampson, of old, shorn of her strong locks, by these unscrupulous Delilahs, and given over to the Philistines, and they have made her to grind in their prison house, unto this day.

42. Likewise, do they seek to put out her two eyes, by destroying her free schools, the pride, and glory, of the Realm, and the chief corner stone, of all her greatness.

43. For with these, will she yet triumph, over all her foes, (at home, and abroad,) but destroy these, and the blackness of darkness, will cover her, as with a pall.

44. Therefore, men of Columbia, look well to your steps, and guard well your liberties; else will the Church of Rome, destroy all, that is worth keeping, for she is the sworn foe, of all civil, and religious liberty, and in darkness, is her habitation.

45. Then say not, that all is well, for there is no safety, for liberty, in any land, where she dwelleth, neither can there be, for liberty of conscience, doth

she abhor.

46. Therefore, when she saith unto you, behold in me, a lovely dwelling place; then shall ye answer, go to, now thou whited sepulcher;—

47. Verily, is Spain, or Mexico, or sunny Italy, a lovely place wherein to dwell, and these are your children.

48. Surely, do your works, speak for themselves, and what ye have made of these Priest-ridden countries, would ye make of Columbia, if ye could.

49. God forbid, that ye should ever get the power, you so much covert, in this free land, for then, would, Columbia, be the delight of the Nations, no more forever.

NOTE.—This description of the people of Ireland, has not been written with any intention to Burlesque, that ancient race; but it is an indisputable fact, that, the emigrants from that unfortunate Isle, who came to America, in the early days of the Republic, (to which time this description is intended to apply), were mostly of that down trodden class, the Peasentry,—and few, if any of them, could read.—sent in many cases, by, and at, the expense of the British Government, simply to get rid of them. But to-day, it is not so, in f ct, those that can rea', form the rule, and not the exception, to-day.

And notwithstanding the warfare waged, by the Church of Rome, against the Public Schools, yet will not all these people, (usually so obedient to her behests) go with her in this matter —vide the l te elections in Ohio,— they having learned, that a good e ucation, not only makes a ma a better citizen, but a better Christian, a'so. Which fact, fully prov s, t' at the Irish Nation, will not be behind any other, in a'l that makes, man-a-man, when given an equal chance to improve. And it also proves the further f ct, that many of them, at least, fully appreciate the value of the free Public schools, in this l ind of their adoption, and the nece sity of keeping them, free from all re igious interferance whatever. Believing that the church, should attend to its l gitimate duties, and not seek to make the education of the youth a Sectarian matter, for of a certainty are the free schools, the head-lights of this great nation. And cursed be the hand, that would destroy them!

CHAPTER XIII.

1. Now it came to pass, after Martin commenced to reign, that the chief men of the south, took council together, and their council, was after this manner.

2. Behold, Andrew, is no longer chief Ruler, but, Martin, reigns in his stead,

3. Now therefore, let us go forward, and do that, which we could not do, in the reign of Andrew; for verily Andrew, was a mighty ruler, and the nations round about feared him greatly.

4. For did he not smite the hosts of the King of Britain, at New Orleans, and drive them from the land; in the reign of James the I, and did he not also smite the Amelakites, of the west and south Provinces, and discomfit them greatly—

5. Yea, and when we did that which was not pleasing, in his sight, in the matter of slavery, did he not cause all our plans to come to naught, and put John, our chief speaker, to shame, in so much, that he fled from the city of Washington, for his life—

6. And did he not say, as the Lord liveth, and he lived, that he would hang John, and put the people of the south to the sword, if they so much as attempted, to do the thing, that was in their hearts, and did not the fear of him come upon all the people of the south provinces—

7. But, Martin, is a man of peace, therefore let us take council, with the men of the north, and peradventure some of them, will come over unto us, and by their help, we shall yet be able, to do all that is in our hearts, against the Black men.

8. For of a certainty, are the Democrats, on our side, likewise, that portion of the Whig party, called Dough faces, (the same meaneth cowards,) will we compel, to join us, and with their help, will me force the north, to give us all that we shall ask.

9. And this council, pleased the men of the south greatly, and they said, now shall we become exceeding great, and have bond men, and bond women, and we will sell them, in the market, like the beasts of the field, and no man shall prevent us.

10. Yea, we will even sell our own children, (of mixed blood) in the city of Washington, the chief city of the realm; selah!

11. For verily, is not this a white man's government; what rights, therefore, have the children of Ham, that we are bound to respect, surely, shall they be our bondman, they, and their children after them, forever.

12. Then, did these wicked men, commence anew, to carry out what they feared to do, in the reign of Andrew, for they feared him, greatly, but they feared not Martin.

13. And, when the Sanhedrim, had again assembled, at Washington, lo, John, and all those that fled in the days of Andrew, came also.

CHAPTER XIV.

1. Now Martin the I, was a man of small ability, exceeding vain, full of deceit and pride, from the province of New York, and of the democratic party.

2. Also, was he called "Reynard, or the fox of Kinderhook," (for it was from that city that he came:) on account of the great craft, and cunning, with which he deceived the people.

3. For he was full of deceit, and duplicity, insomuch, that it was a common saying, among the people, that in that respect, was he like unto the Fox.

4. Verily, had Columbia a sad fall, in the day that Martin became chief ru'er; for in comparison with Andrew, in firmness, boldness, and force of character, he was, as is the Ass! unto the Lion; and from that time on, until the reign of Abraham,(with two exceptions) were her rulers simply contemptible.

5. They being with these two exceptions, wholly controled, by the slave power, each one seeming to strive in all his acts, to please his southern masters, more than had his predecessors, and to sap the foundations of the temple of Liberty, in all that he did.

6. Yea, so thoroughly had the virus of democracy worked in the veins of this political trickster, that in his epistle to the people, when made chief ruler, (called his inaugural) he had the shameless audacity, to characterize the institution of slavery, as both just, expedient, wise, and humane, and proclaimed his fixed determination, to defend it.*

7. And because of this, were the men of the south bold, and defiant, as in former times, for the firm hand of Andrew, was upon them no longer, believing that with Martin, they could do whatsoever they listed.

8. And Martin, spake within himself after this manner, — Behold am not I chief ruler, in Columbia, in place of Andrew, and can I not become as great a ruler as was he, if so be that I please the men of the south.

9. Now therefore will I council with John, called Calhoun, and others of the south provinces, that are for slavery, in the Sanhedrim, and see what would best please them.

10. For peradventure, if I do this, that I shall be made chief ruler for eight years, (for it was the custom in Columbia, that if a ruler pleased the people, for four years, that then would they make him ruler for four years more.)

11. And he sent for John, and his followers, and when they were come

---

*These words actually occured, in Mr. Van Buren's inaugural, which shows to what an abject state of servility the democracy of the north had been reduced, by the pro-slavery party, and for what kind of pottage, they were willing to sell their birthright.

CHAPTER XIV.

before him, he spake unto them after this manner.

12. Behold, I am chief ruler of Columbia, in place of Andrew, and it is my desire, to please the men of the south, in all things.

13. And Richard, whose sir name is Johnson, have the people chosen, to go in, and out before me, and also to stand in my place, in certain times; but the rest of the chiefs, shall I appoint,

14. Therefore tell me now whom ye will that I shall appoint, and it shall be done, for verily, do I greatly desire to please you, in all that I do.

15. And John said unto Martin, what ye say doth please us exceedingly, and these are they, whom ye shall appoint as chiefs, under you.

16. John, whose sir name is Forsyth, shall be chief scribe over the people; Joel, whose sir name is Ponisett, shall be chief in the department of war; Mahlon, whose sir name is Dickinson, shall be over the ships of war; Winfield, shall be captain of the Host; and Levi, whose sir name is Woodbury, shall be over the treasury of the people.

17. This shall ye do, and it shall be well, and if ye will do all things, that we desire in the matter of slavery, then shall ye be chief ruler for eight years.

18. And it came to pass when Martin heard the words of John, that his heart leaped for joy, and he hasted to do as he commanded.

19. Now there was at this time, in the province of Massachusetts, two mighty men, men of renown, and they were in the sanhedrim of the people, at Washington,

20. The name of the one was John, commonly called Quincy, him who had afforetime been chief ruler, and the name of the other was Daniel, sir named the God-like,

21. And they were mighty in the sanhedrim; constantly working for the abolition of Slavery, albeit, Daniel, was not as zealous, as John.

22. And the men of the south were exceeding bitter, against John, and Daniel, for they were the champions of the north, against slavery, therefore were they hated exceedingly, by the men of the south.

23. But John was fearless, and firm, against all the threats of the men of the south, for he was determined, that slavery, should be driven from the land.

24. Yea, no man in all the land of Columbia, was as bold, and fearless, as was John, or as firm for the right.

25 Neither is the memory of any of Columbia's sons, so dear, to the people, except that of George, the first chief ruler, as is that of John, the old man eloquent.

26. Better would it have been for Colmbia, had there been more such as was he, in the sanhedrim, for then, would she needed not, the baptism of blood, that she gat in the Rebellion, as a punishment, for her sins.

27. And the strife was exceeding bitter between the men of the north, and the men of the south, all the days of Martin, which were four years.—

28. For such had been the folly, and imbecility of his reign, that the people of the north, refused to have

him rule over them any longer.

29. For he served his southern masters faithfully, having neither the courage, or disposition, to rule for the best good of all the people, as had Andrew, but his whole aim, was his own personal agrandizement, at the expense of liberty.

30. Now the rest of the acts of Martin, and all that he did, and the trouble that he had with the realm of Britain, in the province of Maine, also in the province of New York, called the Patriot war;

31. Also the zeal, with which he fought for slavery; and against the cause of liberty—

32. Behold, they are written in the book, of the records, of the sanhedrim, at Washington, made during his reign, and the people made, William; chief ruler in his stead, and he commenced to reign.†

33. For the democratic party, had at that time become so corrupt, that their own wickedness, frightened them, therefore did they repent, and do their first works, (for a season,) by helping make William, chief Ruler.

---

† Harrison. 1841.

CHAPTER XV.

1. Now William the I, was a man of war, well known in the realm, of the whig party, and from the province of Indiania.

2. And they gave him John, whose sir name was Tyler, to go in and out before him, and to stand in his place, in certain times; Daniel, whose sir name was Webster, was chief scribe over the people; John, whose sir name was Bell, was chief in the department of war; Abel, whose sir name was Upshir, was over the ships of war; Winfield, was captain of the host; and Thomas, whose sir name was Ewing, was over the treasury of the people.

3. And the people of the north rejoiced greatly, when this was done, for they said in William, and John, had liberty, two mighty champions.

4. For although John was a slave-holder, yet had the men of the north no fears, for they said surely he will not betray us, should he perchance become chief ruler, but they were sadly deceived, in John!

5. Now William, had led the hosts of Columbia, against the Amelekites of the west provinces, in former times and discomfited them greatly, at a place called "Tip Canoe," therefore was he called, "Old Tip-Canoe," by the people; and his fame as a man of war, was in all the land.

6. Moreover he was a statesman, as well as a man of war, on account of which, the people rejoiced the more, because in that, were they doubly armed.

7. But the men of the south, were exceeding wroth, with the men of the north, because William was made chief ruler, for he was for liberty, and not slavery.

8. While the men of the north that loved liberty, rejoiced the more, for now, did they hope, that slavery would be driven from the land, but in this were they again doomed to disappointment—

9. For after a short reign of one month, William the I, slept with his Fathers, and John, became chief ruler in his stead.

10. Yea, many did believe that William the I, had been secretly poisoned, by the men of the south, in order that John, might come to be chief ruler, they well knowing, that in him, slavery had a firm, and steadfast friend.

11. Then did the people mourn, for in William, did Columbia loose a mighty man, and true, and the cause of Liberty, a mighty champion, and the people mourned for William, for many days.

12. Now John the III, was from the Province of Virginia, a man of strong will, and like all his race, ex-

43

ceeding proud, but as a statesman, contemptable—

13. And although elected by northern votes, yet, was his heart with the south, therefore, when he became chief ruler, did the south again come into possession of the government.

14. For he betrayed the men of the north, who had given him his high office, and became a traitor, to the sacred cause of liberty, and brought contempt upon himself, and the realm.

15. Yea, the men of the south did with John, whatsoever they listed, for he was as a reed, in their hands.

16. And the strife was exceeding bitter, all the days of John, which were four years, and the whole land was filled with violence, on account of slavery.

17. But when four years were expired, the people made James the III, chief ruler, in his stead and he commenced to reign.‡

18. Now the acts of John, and all that he did, and how he betrayed the north, and helped to strengthen slavery;

19. Behold they are written in the book, of the records, of the sanhedrim, at Washington, made during his reign, and James reigned in his stead.

‡ Polk, 1845.

CHAPTER XVI.

1. Now James, the III, was like John, the III, and Martin the I, a man of small ability, as a ruler, a friend of slavery, of the democratic party, and from the province of Tennessee.

2. And the democratic party rejoiced exceedingly, inasmuch as the election of James, was a great victory for the slave power.

3. Now the strife at this time, was very bitter, for the reason, that the men of the north, greatly desired that Henry, whose sir name was Clay, should be chief ruler.

4. Now Henry, was one of the mighty ones, of the Realm; eloquent of tongue, had been long in the Sanhedrim, was much beloved by the people, was of the Whig party, and from the province of Kentucky.

5. Moreover, was he a statesman, and a mighty councellor, learned in the Laws, and all that appertained unto the government of the Realm, and in the sanhedrim, was there no man, from the south provinces, that could excel him, or that was preferred before him.

6. Now it had aforetime been in the minds of the men of the north, to make Henry, chief ruler, and had they at this time, acted with wisdom, they would of a certainty, have prevailed.

7. But alas, for the wisdom of the north, they became a house divided, against itself, and were sadly beaten.

8. For, there dwelt in those days, in the city of Cincinnati, a certain man, that was a prophet, whose name was James, of the family of Birney, and he went throughout the north, and became a lying prophet, unto the people, prophesying thus unto them,

9. Follow ye now after me, for I am a chosen vessel, to bring deliverance, unto the slave, therefore, make ye of me, a chief ruler, for ye are able.

10. Whereupon, many were deceived, and followed James, into the wilderness, where they all perished miserably, and Henry, was beaten.

NOTE.—The writer well remembers, the bitterness with which this campaign was conducted. Partizan feeling ran high, and many of the principal cities of the north, had the appearance of a forest, on account of the number of liberty poles erected in them,—Hickory, being emblematic of Polk (or young Hickory, as he was called,) by the democratic party) while the ash, symbolized Mr. Clay,—and over 5 o of these poles were standing in the city of Rochester, N. Y., in the month of October, 184-. And to add to the confusion and increase the excitement, the Millerites, had also, concluded to burn up the world, at that time, never will the writer forget, the meeting he attended at the Agricultural Hall in Rochester, on that eventful 14th of October. This, was to have been the last meeting held on earth, and surely; it ought to have been the last, that any of those fanatics, ever held outside of a mad-house.

Note.—James G. Birney, who the abolition party, ran as an independent candidate, which *insane folly*, caused the defeat of Mr. Clay.

11. For although Henry was himself a slave-holder, yet was he known to be a just man, therefore would not the men of the south vote for him, and without their help, he could not prevail.

12. For so determined were these men to extend slavery, and perpetuate it, that no man, (except he was such an one, as they could use,) had any chance to become chief ruler of Columbia.

13. Therefore was it, that men who were contemptable, in every way and who also brought contempt upon the people, were made chief rulers, because the south could use them.

14. For not only were these men determined that slavery, should extend over all the soil that Columbia then owned; but they also contemplated making war upon the nations round about, in order to extend its dominion.

15. Now there is a part of Columbia, that lieth west of the great River, called Mississippi, and south of the river called Red, that is at this day, known as the province of Texas.

16. And this land, was in former times called New Spain; for the King of Spain had planted colonies, therein, three hundred years ago, and also in the land called Mexico.

17. But at length, the King of Spain was driven from Mexico, by the people, and that beautiful land became a Republic.

18. Albeit, the new government was more despotic, (if such a thing could be,) than was that of the King; for the people were Catholics, and wholly under the rule of their priests.

19. And this bondage had been exceeding cruel and oppressive, until the people were sunk in degredation, so deep, that Mexico, although a beautiful land, was the worst of all lands, wherein to dwell.—

20. —For there was no law, but the law of the Church, also was the land, and money of the realm, nearly all in its possession, or under its control, in consequence of which the inhabitants of that fair land, were in a hard place.

21. Now Mexico claimed the land called Texas, and had appointed Governors therefor, for many long years, but after Columbia had purchased New France, she also claimed Texas as a part, of her purchase, and sought to take possession thereof.

22. —For Texas, is an exceeding large land, and fair; and the people of Columbia desired much to occupy it, but the rulers of Mexico, would not permit them.

23. Therefore came it to pass, that there was war and tumult in the land, for the men of Columbia, that went to Texas, were continually fighting with the armies of Mexico, that were sent against them, which kept the whole realm in a state of war, for many years.

24. Now there were in Columbia, at that time, many wicked men, also many that were in debt, or that had broken the laws, and many of these from fear of punishment, had fled to Texas.

25. And the land, was full of men, that like the men of David, in the reign of Saul, King of Israel; owed every man his neighbor, or that had committed some crime.

26. Men that carried their lives in their hand, and were both ready and willing to take the life of any that should oppose them, in any wickedness that they thought to do.

27. (Albeit, there were many that were good men, and true, at that time, in Texas; nevertheless, it was a land of violence and bloodshed, as it is at this day.)

28. Now, these restless, and lawless men, were continually at war, with the people of Mexico, from the reign of James the II, to the reign of Martin the I, after which the land had rest from war, for a short space.

29. But it came to pass, after James the III, was firmly seated on the Throne, that the men of the south took fresh courage, and they spake unto James after this manner!

30. —Behold, now have we made of you, a chief ruler of Columbia, in place of John, not because ye are worthy, (for ye are not,) but because we have need of you.

31. And by our strategy have the people chosen George, whose sir name, is Dallas, to go in and out before you, and also to stand in your place, (should ye not obey us,) and these are they that shall be chiefs, under you, for we have need of them, also,

32. —James, whose sir name is Buchanan, shall ye make chief scribe, over the people; William, whose sir name is Marcy, shall be your chief in the department of war; George, whose sir name is Bancroft, shall ye put over the ships of war; Winfield, shall be captain of the host, and Robert, whose sir name is Walker, shall ye put over the treasury of the people.

33. —And James said it is well, what ye command, that will I do, for thy servant is not the man to disobey his masters.

34. Now after James had done all these things, it came to pass, that the chief men of the south, spake thus unto the people.

35. —Why stand we here idle, while the men of the north, are setting snares for us continually, in order to destroy slavery,

36. —Adding continually to the number of Provinces, in which there shall be no slavery, by which if we bestir not ourselves, will our power in the Sanhedrim, depart from us, and we ourselves, become slaves.

37. Have ye not observed the land of Texas, that it is a large and goodly land, in the which groweth not only cotton, but also the cane, from which to make the sugar, and that it is in every way adapted to slavery.

38. Let us now compel James, to make war upon Mexico, and peradventure we shall be able to compel the rulers of that land, to give us Texas, for a possession, for behold, all things are now ready.

39. (For Mexico, did still claim Texas, as a part of their country, neither would they consent, that the men of Columbia, should dwell therein.)

40. And this council pleased all the men of the south provinces, and they did compel James to make war upon the land of Mexico, to subdue it.

41. And he gave command to Winfield, and Winfield gat his armies together, and gat him to the land of Mexico, an exceeding great army.

42. And the hosts of Columbia, fought against the hosts of Mexico, and discomfited them, and they became subject unto Columbia; albeit, they maintained a separate government; but the land of Texas, became a part of Columbia,

43. Then did the hosts of Columbia, return unto their own land, and there was peace once more, nevertheless, the land was filled with mourning, on account of the men slain in the war.

44. Now the reign of James, had not been pleasing unto the men of the north, on account of the war, with Mexico, and after four years were expired, they made Zachary, chief ruler, in his stead, and he commenced to reign.†

45. Now, the acts of James, and all that he did, and the wars that he had with the realm of Mexico, and the help, that was given to the slave power thereby, and his betrayal of the cause of liberty,

46. Behold, they are all written in the Book of the Records, of the Sanhedrim, at Washington, made during his reign, called the History of the War with Mexico, for the acquisition of Texas, and Zachary reigned in his stead.

---

† Taylor, 1849.

CHAPTER XVII.

1. Now Zachary the I, was a mighty man of war from his youth, much beloved by the people of the whole realm, of the Whig or Republican party, and from the Province of Mississippi.

2. Also, was he the chief of the captains under Winfield, when the hosts of Columbia, made war, upon the land of Mexico.

3. And the victory was sure, for the men of Columbia, when Zachary led them, for he was well versed in all the arts of war.

4. Likewise, was he called old rough and ready, by the men of the army; albeit, his heart was tender, even, like unto that of a little child.

5. Now the boldness of the men of the south, in compelling James to make war upon Mexico, in order that they might thereby acquire new territory, over which to extend slavery, (for, for that, and that alone, was it made,) had opened the eyes of many, of the Democratic party in the north, to their danger.

6. Therefore, did they a second time join hands with the whigs, in the election of Zachary, hoping thereby, not only to please the south,—

7. —But, that this act of repentance, would also make the whigs less, watchful and vigilent, at which the whigs were greatly rejoiced.—

8. Saying one to the other, peradventure the eyes of these men, are now opened, that they may behold all the wickedness, of these Traffickers in human flesh, before it is too late, and sin no more.

9. And they gave him Millard, whose sir name was Fillmore, to go in and out before him, and to stand in his place, in certain times; Daniel, whose sir name was Webster, was chief scribe over the people; George, whose sir name was Crawford; was chief in the department of war; William, whose sir name was Preston, was over the ships of war; Winfield, was captain of the host; and William, whose sir name was Meredith, was over the Treasury of the people.

10. And it came to pass, when Zachary commenced to reign, that the people of the south provinces, rejoiced greatly, saying, surely is the Lord on our side, for have we not discomfited the people of Mexico, and taken their land for a possession,

11. —And will not that strengthen us, against the north, by giving us more slave territory, and is not Zachary, one of us; verily, shall we now be able, to do all, that is in our hearts,

against the black man,—Selah.

12. And the clank of the chain, and the crack of the drivers whip, shall again be heard over all the realm of Columbia,

13. —And when the Sanhedrim, were again assembled, they spake unto the men of the north after this manner.

14. Behold now, if ye will consent that all that part of Columbia, that lieth west of a certain river, and south of a certain line, (to be named by us) shall be slave territory, then will we live at peace with you, but if ye will not, then shall ye surely have war.‡

15. But the men of the north, said nay, this thing shall not be done, neither will we make any compromise with you touching this matter.

16. For have we not already made two compromises with you, and ye will not abide by either of them, neither would ye abide by this one, should we make it.

17. Surely, ye shall not go into the land ye speak of, with your slaves, but freemen shall dwell therein, and no other, forever; there shall be no slaves there—

18. For, notwithstanding that ye have conquered Mexico, and obtained Texas for a possession, ye shall never go into the land ye speak of with your slaves.

19. For with Zachary, for chief ruler, liberty is safe, and if ye so much as attempt to do this thing, that is in your hearts, ye shall surely be put to shame.

20. But, alas for the men of the north, they were again doomed to disappointment, their hopes blasted, and liberty was again to recieve another check—

21. For after a short reign of one year and four months, Zachary the I, slept with his Fathers, and Millard became chief ruler in his stead.

22. And there was great mourning, for Zachary, and the mourning continued for many days.‖

---

‡NOTE.—The matter referred to in this place, was the compromise, (or Omnibus) Bill of Mr. Clay's, brought forward at this time, and defeated. But after the death of President Taylor, it was again taken up, and was after its discussion had caused much strife in Congress, finally passed and became the law of the land, including the infamous fugitive Slave Bill, recieving the signiture of President Millard Fillmore, in the month of August, 1850. This Bill which was to make Kansas, a Slave State, completely abrogated the compromise of 1820. But thanks to the liberty loving men of the north, it could not be enforced and in the end, Kansas became a Free State.

‖ NOTE.—A certain amount of fatality seemed to attach to the whig party at that time, the death of Mr. Harrison in one short month after his inauguration caused many of the people to think that he had been poisoned, particularly when taken in connection with the policy adopted and carried out by Mr. Tyler, his successor, and when a second whig President was elected in the person of Mr. Taylor, an his death following so quickly, many were ready to charge the south with their murder, whether this was so or not, will never be known in this world, but it was certainly a little singular, that the only Presidents that died in office were both whigs, and uncompromising enemies of slavery. And when we consider, the stake, that the south were playing for, it might be cause for suspicion of foul play.

CHAPTER XVIII.

1. Now Millard the I, was of the whig or republican party, had been long in the Sanhedrim, well versed in all the laws of the realm, and from a northern province, even that of New York,

2. —Therefore did the people say, now will liberty still be safe, for Millard is one of us, and we need have no fear that he will betray us, as did John whose sir name was Tyler, and they took courage.

3. Now there were many of the men of the south, that in their hearts rejoiced exceedingly, that Zachary was dead, for they were not long in discovering that he, like Andrew, had a will of iron, and a firm hand, which would of a certainty keep them in check,

4. And on account of this, was it that their hearts failed them; when they saw his firmness, and knew that not only was he not with them, but that in him, they had a master.

5. But after Millard became chief ruler, it came to pass, that their courage came again, and they spake among themselves after this manner.

6. Behold, Zachary sleeps with his Fathers, and Millard reigns in his stead, now therefore let us go forward and do that, which we could not do while he was upon the Throne, for verily, in firmness and vigilance, was he even as was Andrew.

7. But Millard is not so, therefore let us speak softly unto him, and peradventure we can deceive him, and they spake unto Millard after this manner,—

8. Lo, Zachary sleeps with his Fathers, and ye are chief ruler in his stead, now therefore, if ye will be one of us, and aid us in obtaining all that we desire in the matter of slavery—

9. —Then shall ye of a certainty be chief ruler for eight years, and shall get exceeding much spoil and riches, behold, we have said it,

10. —But if ye will not do all that we desire, then shall ye come to naught, and your house made a dung hill; for we are determined to control this government, and slavery shall yet extend over all the land,

11. —And Millard consented to all that the south required of him, — betrayed the party that made him chief ruler, and sold himself to the enemies of liberty.

12. Then was there great rejoicing in the south, at what Millard had done, and great mourning at the north, for the thing was very grievous unto the people of the north that were against slavery;

13. —Now after Millard had done all this, it came to pass, that the chief

men of the south again took council among themselves, and their council was after this manner;

14. —Surely has the set time come, that we have so long wished for, and now will we have a law in favor of slavery, that shall make the ears of all that shall hear of it to tingle,—Selah,

15. For Zachary, (who we could not rule,) sleeps with his Fathers; but with Millard, can we do whatsoever we list, for he is as a reed in our hands,

16. —And now, this stone which through the stubbornness of Zachary was rejected, shall by the treachery of Millard, become the head of the corner,

17. —Therefore, let us now find a man from the north, to go before us, and aid us to pass the bill called the compromise, (in the attempt to pass which we were aforetime beaten by the firmness of Zachary,)

18. —For peradventure, if the north see their chief men, willing to do this thing, that then shall they fear to oppose us, and thus shall we of a certainty prevail.

19. And they chose Stephen, (who is also called Arnold,) to do this thing, for he was of the democratic party, the party that favored slavery, (albeit, there were many true men in that party that were for freedom,) nevertheless, it was the slave holders party.

20. Now Stephen, was a man small in statue, but of a giant intellect, was the leader of the democratic party in the north, well versed in the laws of the land, and he was the chief speaker for his party in the Sanhedrim, at Washington.

21. And they said unto Stephen, if now ye will aid us in the passage of the Omnibus Bill, so that it become the law of the realm, then shall ye surely be made chief ruler of Columbia after Millard, and shall become exceeding great in the land.

22. And the thing pleased Stephen, and he said unto them, what ye say, that will thy servant do, for this thing pleaseth thy servant, (for Stephen, was ambitious, and the desire of his heart was to be chief ruler of Columbia.)

23. And from that hour, Stephen walked no more with the north, but went over to the south, body and soul, and he became their champion.

24. And from that time forth, was the contest upon this matter, exceeding fierce and violent in the Sanhedrim, for the men of the north, (that loved liberty,) were determined that this great wickedness should not be done

25. But alas for the men of the north, they were compelled to fight this battle, without their former great captain, in consequence of which, they were beaten.

26. For John, (the old man eloquent) slept with his Fathers, after a long and glorious public life, without a stain upon his great name, for he, like his illustrious father, was a true man, and had stood valiantly for liberty.

27. —And his mantle had fallen upon Daniel, (the great expounder,) now the people of the north, had great faith in Daniel, for he had been long in the Sanhedrim, and had fought many a battle by the side of John, in

CHAPTER XVIII.

the cause of Liberty, and against slavery; (but a great change had come upon Daniel, since the death of John.¶)

28. Now there was a sickness, that prevailed in the land every four years, (called the Ruler's fever,) and it came to pass that Daniel, was smitten with this disease.

29. And it was told unto the chief men of the south, that Daniel was sick with the Ruler's fever, and it rejoiced them greatly.

30. And they said surely is the hand of the Lord in this, and now shall we get Daniel, to come over unto us, and the north shall be left without a champion.

31. And they sent messengers unto him, to know if he would be recovered of his sickness, and the messengers came into the presence of Daniel.

32. And when Daniel saw the messengers, he said unto them, from whence come ye, and what seek ye in this place, for I know you not!

33. And the messengers said unto him, thy servants are from the south provinces, and were sent by our masters, to ask after thy health, for it hath been told in the south provinces, that ye have the Rulers fever—

34. Therefore were we sent, for our masters greatly desire thy recovery, and if ye will take the remedy, that we shall offer unto you, (which groweth only in the south provinces) then shall ye recover, but if ye will not, then shall ye surely die.

35. And Daniel said, what is the remedy, that ye will give unto me, for surely I would recover of this disease.—

36. And they said unto Daniel, if you will aid Stephen to pass the bill, that we desire, so that it become the law of the realm, then shall ye recover of this sickness,

37. And we will make you chief ruler after Millard, (for no man can be chief ruler of Columbia, unless we make him so,) and this is the remedy that ye must take, if ye would recover of this sickness.

38. Then said Daniel, unto them peradventure, if I do this, that I shall not recover, for did not John the III, and James the III, take your medicine, when they were sick with this disease, and surely, it recovered not them,

39. And they answered Daniel after this manner, John and Millard were not sick unto death, but ye will surely die, if ye take not the remedy, but if ye will, then shall ye surely be made chief ruler, and they sware unto him.

40. Then in an evil hour, did Daniel consent to all that the messengers required of him, and the bill became the law of the realm, but alas for Daniel, he recovered not of his disease, for the south refused to make him chief ruler.

41. And when the people of the north, were told what Daniel had done there was great lamentation, and they exclaimed, alas! alas! who shall stand

¶Note.—This great and good man who for so many years held aloft the banner of Freedom in Columbia, was while addressing the Speaker of the House of Representatives, at Washington, smitten with appoplexy, Feb., 21, 1848, carried into the Speaker's private room, where he lingered in a partially unconscious state, until the 23d, when he expired. His last words being—*This is the last of Earth; I am content.—What a glorious end, to a well-spent life.*

for Liberty, now that Daniel has fallen from his high place.

42. Now when Daniel saw that the men of the south had decieved him, it came to pass that his heart was broken and he exclaimed, alas! that I should have done this.

43. Verily, hath my desire to be made chief ruler, proved the cause of my ruin, for this foolish act, hath of a certainty destroyed me.

44. —Covering all my former glorious record, as with a pall, would to God! that I had been as true as John, then would my end have been like his.

45. And he gat him to his own province, to a place called Marshfield, and he died there, and was buried, and the people mourned for Daniel, but not as they mourned for John.

46. Nevertheless, the memory of Daniel, and the mighty things that he did in Columbia, shall never fade from the minds of the people, unto the latest generation.§

47. For he was in truth, a mighty councellor, and a mighty man; and

not until the desire to be chief ruler, had clouded his vision, had he ever proved unworthy; or betrayed the liberties of the people.

48. And the strife, was exceeding bitter, all the days of Millard between the north, and the south; for the men of the south, were continually chasing their slaves, that had escaped into the north provinces, to take them back to bondage, and the whole land, was filled with violence,

49. —But the men of the north, would not aid them in their capture, neither would they suffer them, to take them back into bondage, if by any possibility they could prevent it.

50. And the men of the south, said unto the men of the north; behold now if ye do not aid us, or if ye assist the slave, in any manner, even so much as to give him a cup of cold water,

51. —Then shall ye pay unto us, one thousand pieces of silver, and be put in prison, for the space of six months, for such, is the law.

52. But when the men of the north, heard the words of the slave hunters, they were filled with rage, and they exclaimed with one voice,

53. —Are the people dogs, that they should do this, surely, shall this law not be enforced, in this land, neither will we obey it.‖

54. And when four years were expired, the people made Franklin chief ruler, in place of Millard, and great was the rejoicing in the north, that his reign was ended.

55. For it had been more disastrous to the cause of liberty, than had that of

---

§Note.—The end of this truly great man, should be a warning to all, of the evils of ambition. He had long occupied a high place in the councils of the nation, and in the hearts of the people. But the tempting bait held out to him by the leaders of the pro-slavery party, clouded his mind to such an extent, that he fell. But no true American, can ever doubt, that when consenting to use his great name and prestige, in the cause of the south.—That he meant it for the best, thinking it would prevent a civil war. But he quickly saw his great mistake, and surely no man in America, has, (or could lament it, more than did Mr. Webster, himself, for when he saw the full devilishness of the thing, his great manly heart, was broken, and he sank under the load of shame, and remorse, that this act had brought upon him until death came to his relief. Nevertheless, he has left a glorious memory, in Columbia and his like will not; perhaps be seen again for many generations.

CHAPTER XVIII.

any of his predecessors, filling the whole land with turmoil and strife unto its end.

56. Now the acts of Millard, and all that he did, and his betrayal of the north, and the aid that he gave to the slave power

57. —Behold, they are all written in the Book of the Records, of the Sanhedrim, at Washington, made during his reign, and Franklin§ reigned in his stead.

[NOTE.—This infamous law, that for pure nadulterated cussidness, has never been equall·d, contained all the provisions, stated in the text, there is certainly nothing on record, in this, or any other country, that can compare wi·h it, in fiendishness, or cruelty. And to our shame be it said, that the honor of making blood hounds, of her people, was first conferred in free America. No wonder that it could not be enforced, for the execution of it, was so revolting, that very few men, could be found, who could be induced to attempt it, its paternity is not certainly known, although Mr. Mason of Virginia, is charged with begetting it. But at all events, let whoever it was, have all the glory, it was attached, as the tail is to a kite, to the Omnibus Bill, and in that way, became a law. But like the tail of the asp, it contained a terrible sting, fatal, to all it pierced. God forbi·¹, that America, shall ever be cursed, with its like again.

§Pierce, 1853.

CHAPTER XIX.

1. Now Franklin the I., was a man of small ability; very vain, much given to boasting, exceeding fond of strong waters; and as a ruler, contemptible; of the democratic party, and from a northern province, even that of New Hampshire.

2. And he was also a captain, under Winfield, when the hosts of Columbia, wared against Mexico, and took it, but he gat him no renown, as a man of war.

3. And there was great rejoicing in the south, and among the pro-slavery men, of the north, when he was made chief ruler, insomuch, that the whole realm was shaken, from one extremity unto the other, on account of the rejoicing.

4. —For now, they said, do we stand upon a firm foundation, and our borders shall be greatly enlarged, and our gates, strengthened, neither will we fear the men of the north, any more forever,—Selah,

5. —For is not Stephen with us, and doth not he hold, the men of the north, (that are of the democratic party,) in his hand, and hath not the Bill called the Compromise, through him also, become the law of the realm,

6. —Which Bill, hath given us not only the possession, of all the present realm of Columbia, but it giveth us also the possession of all that may be hereafter acquired for slavery.—

7. And hath not the fugitive slave Bill also become the law of the land, whereby we can follow, and recover our slaves, when they shall escape, neither is there any more a man in all the north, that can in any wise deliver them out of our hand.

8. Verily, have our hands, been greatly strengthened, by the treachery of Millard, whereby, he hath done great things for us, but with Franklin for chief ruler, shall we be able to fully complete the good work, that Millard began, surely, is the hand of the Lord in this.

9. And it came to pass, after Franklin was firmly seated upon the throne, that the chief men of the south spake unto him after this manner,

10. Behold now you are chief ruler of Columbia, in place of Millard, because it was our pleasure to make you such,

11. —And if you will truly do all that we desire, then shall it be well with you, and you shall surely be chief ruler, for eight years,

12. —But if ye will not, then shall swift destruction o'er take you, and you shall come to naught, for we are of a certainty fully determined, to rule this land, peaceably if we can, forci-

CHAPTER XIX.

bly if we must;

13. —And this law, that the men of the north, curse so deeply, will we surely compel them to obey, in all its provisions, (through you.)

14. Lo, have we not already compelled the return of one Thomas Seemes, from the chief city, of the province of Massachusetts, even the great city of Boston, and was not the fear of us, upon all the inhabitants of that proud city,

15. And have we not also done the same in divers of the north provinces, yea, neither will we stay our hand, until the whole realm, obey us, as in former times.

16. And have we not also, by the treachery of Millard, (and the folly of Daniel,) beaten the north in the matter of Kansas, and obtained it for a possession,—

17. —Yea; and is not Wilson whose sir name is Shannon, governor of that goodly land, and will he not do all the things that we shall require of him.

18. Now, as the Lord liveth, will we make of it a slave province, for its soil is well adapted to the growing of cotton, and corn, in abundance.

19. (Now Kansas, was not yet a province, but was the common heritage of all the provinces, that the rulers, had bought of the Amelekites, that formerly occupied the same, for a possession.)

20. Then said Franklin, what ye council, that will I do, for it is certainly my desire to please you in all things, therefore tell me now all that is in your hearts, for verily in me ye have a true friend.

21. Then said they unto him, this is what ye shall do, if ye would please us,—

22. Lo, we have given you William, whose sir name is King, to go in and out before you, and also to stand in your place, (should ye not do all that we desire,) and these are they, who shall be chiefs under you;

23. William, whose sir name is Marcy, shall be chief scribe over the people; Jefferson whose sir name is Davis, shall be chief in the department of war; James whose sir name is Dobbins, shall be over the ships of war; Winfield, shall be captain of the host; and James, whose sir name is Gurthrie, shall be over the treasury of the people.

24. This do, and it shall be well, and if ye will truly and faithfully do all things, that we shall ask, then of a certainty will we make you chief ruler for eight years, and ye shall become exceeding great in Columbia.

25. And Franklin did all the things the south required of him, for he like Stephen was very ambitious,—

26. —And sold himself to the men of the south, for the promise, of a mess of pottage, but he gat not the pottage.

27. Yea, as it was with Millard, and Daniel, so came it to pass, with Franklin, for he had planted thorns, and he gathered therefrom thistles.

28. Now the men of the south, had gat them to Kansas, in the reign of Millard, thinking thereby to forestall the men of the north, in its possession.

29. And there was no man went, that

was not both ready, and willing, to take the life of any, that should oppose them, verily, they were sons of Belial, one and all.

30. And when it was told in the north, what the men of the south, had done, it came to pass, that there was great indignation; and the people said one to the other, what is this, that the men of the south have done, in that they have gone to Kansas to possess it,

31. — Was it not the agreement made in the days of our fathers, that this was not to be done, surely are these men determined to destroy liberty in Columbia,

32. —Neither is there any trust to be placed in them, for they have broken every covenant, made as to this matter, and are determined to carry slavery into Kansas.

33. Surely, as the Lord liveth, they shall not do this thing, there shall be no slavery in that land, for we will make of it a province, where freemen shall dwell, and no other, there shall be no slaves there,—Selah.

34. Then did the men of the north, get them to Kansas, and the strife commenced for its possession, and it was exceeding bitter; but the men of the north, led by James, whose sir name was Lane, did valliantly, and the victory was finally with the north.

35. Nevertheless the whole realm, was filled with violence, on account of it, all the days of Franklin, even unto the end of his reign, and many were slain, both of the men of the north, and the men of the south,—

36. —Until the whole land was filled with mourning on account of the number of the men, that were slain in Kansas.

37. But the victory was finally with the north, notwithstanding, that Franklin, and Stephen, did work continually for the south, yet they could not prevail;

38. —And violence and anarchy, prevailed throughout the realm, and in the Sanhedrim, all the days of Franklin.

39. Yea, so fierce and bold, had the men of the south became, that no man could speak against slavery, in the south, or in the Sanhedrim, except he took his life in his hand, throughout his reign.

40. And Charles one of the chief men of the Sanhedrim, from the province of Massachusetts, was beaten therein, with stripes; for speaking against slavery.†

41. But at the end of four years, when the people again came to elect a new chief ruler, it came to pass, that there was great excitement in the land of Columbia,—

42. For the rulers fever, again prevailed in all the realm, and Franklin was sick with this disease, and he sent for the southern doctors, to recover him of his sickness.

43. And when they were come unto him, he enquired of them concerning the remedy that grew in the south

---

†NOTE.—This brutal assault, upon Mr. Sumner, by Preston C. Brooks, of South Carolina, was the natural sequence, of the spirit that slavery engenders in the human heart. Yet this bold act, did not fully open the eyes of the north, to their danger.—From this assault, Mr. Sumner never fully recovered.

provinces, and if it would recover him of his fever.

44. And they answered him after this manner; peradventure ye can recover, nevertheless, we know of a certainty, that ye will surely die, for this remedy worketh not the second time.

45. And Franklin said unto them, did ye not certainly say unto me, that if I would do all in my power, as chief ruler, for the extension of slavery, that ye would recover me of the rulers fever, should it come upon me a second time, and that ye would make me chief ruler for four years more

46. —And have I not done all that ye asked of me, yea, and more also, now therefore what is this, that ye say unto me, that I shall surely die, for your medicine, worketh not the second time—

47. Now therefore do I know that ye are liars, and the children of your father the Devil, and his works will ye do, verily, whosoever trusteth in you, shall surely be put to shame.

48. Then Franklin turned his face to the wall, and wept bitterly, and he said surely my punishment is just, for have I not done all in power, to destroy liberty, and strengthen slavery, verily; the way of the transgressor is hard.

49. Then Franklin, got him to his own province, unto a place called Concord, and he died there, and was buried, and the people mourned not for Franklin, for his reign had been inglorious.

50. For he betrayed the men of the north, went over body and soul, to the slave party, sold himself for a mess of pottage, and gat not the pottage.

51. Thus was the sacred cause of liberty, again sacrificed, upon the altar of ambition, and the chains of the bondmen strengthened, by this northern dough-face, that the people of the north, in their insane folly, had helped to make chief ruler.

52. Now all the acts of Franklin, and the evil that he did to the cause of liberty, and his betrayal of the north, and the disgrace that he brought upon himself, and the realm, in consequence of his wickedness and folly—

53. Behold, they are written in the Book of the Records, of the Sanhedrim, at Washington, made during his reign, and the people made James, chief ruler, in his stead, and he commenced to reign.‡

---

‡Buchannan, 1857.

CHAPTER XX.

1. Now James the IV., was old, and well stricken in years, he was moreover a man of no ability, contemptible in every way as a ruler, even more so than was Franklin, whose reign had been so disastrous, to the cause of liberty, from the province of Pennsylvania, and of the democratic party.

2. And it rejoiced the men of the south greatly, when he was made chief ruler, for they said, he sha'l be as a reed in our hands, surely did we do well, with Franklin, but with James will we gain much more, for with him, of a certainty, can we do whatsoever we list—

3. And they said unto James, behold we have made you chief ruler of Columbia, in place of Franklin.

4. John, whose sir name is Breckenridge, have we chosen to go in and out before you, and also to stand in your place, in certain times, and these are they, whom we would have you appoint as chiefs, under you.

5. Lewis, whose sir name is Cass, shall be chief scribe over the people; John, whose sir name is Floyd, shall be chief in the department of war; Isaac, whose sir name is Toucy, shall be over the ships of war; Winfield shall be captain of the host; and Howell, whose sir name is Cobb, shall be over the treasury of the people.

6. And James, did all the things that the south required of him, for he was on their side, moreover, he was like a reed, in the hands of their leaders.

7. Now there had been in the Sanhedrim, of the people at Washington, in the days of John, the old man eloquent; and Daniel, the great expounder; two mighty men from the south provinces, men of renown.

8. The name of the one was Henry, (him whom the men of the north, aforetime, sought to make chief ruler,) and the name of the other, was Thomas, whose sir name was Benton, from the province of Missouri, and they were both mighty in the Sanhedrim, and also among the people—

9. And they, together with John, called Calhoun, had been the champions of the south, in the Sanhedrim, all the days of John and Daniel; and had helped to make all the laws, touching slavery, but Henry was the noblest of the three.

10. Now Henry had been greatly beloved, for the justness, and fairness with which his whole public life was marked, notwithstanding, he was from a slave holding province, and did himself hold slaves.

11. Likewise, was he called by the people, the war horse of Kentucky, on account of the zeal, and courage,

CHAPTER XX.

he displayed in the strife between the north and the south, in the matter of slavery, always to be found in the front of the battle.¶

12. Also was Thomas, well liked by the people, for he was a man of great intellect, and firm for what he conceived to be right, and on account of his great love, for a specie currency for the realm, was called by the people old bullion,

13. —While John, called Calhoun, fought continually, for the extension of slavery over the whole land, and was the prime cause of all the trouble in the realm, on account of it.

14. And he would have plunged the nation in a civil war long before the reign of Abraham the I, except he had been prevented by the firmness of Andrew, as before stated, supported by Henry and Thomas.

15. Now Henry and John, both slept with their father's and their mantles, had fallen upon unworthy men, even Sons of Belicl, and it was on account of their folly and corruption, that the realm was plunged in civil war.

16. For there was no Henry, to hold them in check in the south, or a.

John to council wisdom and firmness in the north, and their places, could no man fill.—

17. Therefore was it that contention and violence, prevailed both in the Sanhedrim, and among the people, until Columbia became a reproach among the nations round about, on account of the wickedness, and folly of her rulers.

18. For the war, for the possession, of Kansas, had resulted as before stated in the defeat of the south, in consequence of which their chief men were in a fearful rage—

19. And from that time forth, did they commence to plot the destruction of the government, and to form one in its place, based upon slavery, and in the which, that should be the chief corner stone.

20. Their hearts seemingly, set on fire of hell, and filling the whole land with turmoil—

21. Neither did they in any manner seek to conceal their wicked designs, from the people of the north, who they in their foolish pride, derided as paltroons, and cowards.

22. —Saying that one of their number could chase a thousand, and that two could put ten thousand to flight.—

23. Standing openly in the Sanhedrim, and defying the men of the north, and that no man should be chief ruler, except he was of their choice.—

24. Filling the whole realm with violence, and breathing out threatenings and wrath continually, until the second year of the reign of James.

¶Note.—Few men in any country, were ever in public life as long as Henry Clay, or that passed throngh so much as did he, in the discharge of what he conceived to be his duty to the whole country. He was in ability inferior to no one of his t me, and had in fact very few peers, in this, or any other country. Born a slave holder, and always representing a slave holding constituency, and living in a time, when the subject was constantly before the people, yet his course, in the m tter, was such, as to command the confidence, and respect, of ti e bitterest foes of that sum of all Villainies. Had th : south more like him, she would not be in the condition she is to-day. Peace to his Memory.

CHAPTER XXI.

1. And it came to pass, in the second year of the reign of James the IV., in the tenth month, on the sixteenth day of the month, that John, (commonly called Old John Brown,) made war upon the south, with an army of two and twenty men.

2. And he went up against one of the strong holds of the south, in the province of Virginia, called Harpers Ferry, in the night watch, and fought against it, and took it; now the number of inhabitants at that place, was about five thousand.

3. And in the morning, when the sun was risen, the people looked, and behold, they were prisoners, and there was also five score thousand stand of arms, besides munitions of war, in that place,

4. —For not only had John called Floyd, (who was chief in the department of war,) filled all the strong holds of the south, with arms and munitions of war for the people of the south to use in the defence of slavery.—

5. But the former rulers of Columbia had erected at that place, exceeding great buildings, in the which to manufacture arms, and munitions of war for the realm, (therefore was it a notable place, and of great importance to the realm.)

6. Now when it was told unto Henry, (commonly called Old Vanity,) who was governor of that province, that John was in possession of Harpers Ferry, it came to pass that his knees smote together, and his countenance was changed, and he became like one dead.

7. For John was known to be exceeding bold, in the cause of liberty, and against slavery, insomuch that the whole south stood in fear of him.

8. —Surely (at that time) was there no man in all the land, as fearless as was John, and the whole realm was in commotion on account of him,

9. But when it was told unto Henry, that John had but two and twenty men, his spirit came again, and he gat together his army, even five thousand fighting men.‡

10. And he gat him to Harpers Ferry, to war against John, and the army of Henry, encompassed the army of John, round about, and they put the battle in array.

11. And Henry said unto his army, be strong now, and of good courage, and peradventure the Lord will give us the victory, therefore acquit yourselves like men,—

12. And they fought against John, and took him, and there fell of the army of John, seventeen men; and of the army of Henry, seven; for John

‡Henry A. Wise.

CHAPTER XXI.

and his men did valiently, and showed themselves to be men of war,—

13. And Henry hanged John, at Charlestown, in that province, and the men of the south rejoiced greatly, when this was done, for the fear of him, was upon all the people of the south provinces.

14. Now the hanging of John, caused great excitement in the north, insomuch, that scarcely any other matter was spoken of for many days.

15. And the men of the north said, O that Andrew I., was chief ruler, in place of James, for then would these rebels quickly find that the wages of sin, is death, but James is as a reed, in their hands.

16. And from that hour were they determined that slavery should extend no farther in Columbia, and that no man who was not its deadly foe, should ever again be made chief ruler.

17. And it came to pass, at the end of three years, when the people came to elect, a new chief ruler, that there was great commotion in the land,

18. —For Stephen, (some time called Arnold,) John called Breckenridge; and William, whose sir name was Seward; were all sick, with the Ruler's fever,

19. —And the men of the north, called a council at the city of Chicago, to consult as to who should be made chief ruler in the place of James, and the friends of William, were exceeding zealous in his behalf, but they could not prevail.

20. Now William, was of the whig, or republican party, and was mighty in the Sanhedrim of the people, even as had been Daniel, and John, and was the champion of the north, (albeit, he was not as true to liberty, or as firm against slavery, as was John.)

21. And the men of the south, said unto the men of the north, now if ye will make Stephen, chief ruler, and will also give a pledge, that ye will carry out the law, called the Fugitive Slave Law, then will we stay in the Union;

22. —But if ye do not, then will we destroy this government, and make a new one, in which slavery shall be the chief corner stone.

23. But the people of the north, said nay, Stephen shall not be chief ruler, neither shall your law be enforced in this land, for we are not dogs, neither are we devils, if ye are.

24. Then was the strife exceeding bitter, and although Stephen took the the medicine, of the southern doctors freely, and they also called a council, on his case at Charleston, at which all the quack slavery doctors from the north were called, yet, they could not recover Stephen, of his fever.

25. And when Stephen saw that he could not recover, he was sick at heart, and he exclaimed, this alas; is the end of a misspent life,—

26. O, that I had fought as zealously for liberty, as I have for slavery, for then, would my name have been honored in the land; verily he that consenteth with sinners, shall surely be put to shame.

27. Then Stephen gat him to his

own province, to the City of Chicago, (the meaning whereof is it stinketh,) and he died there, and was buried, and no man that loved liberty mourned for Stephen, and the people chose Abraham, for the next chief ruler in Columbia,

28. —Not being willing to make William chief ruler, as he was not as firm for liberty, as Abraham, nevertheless, he was greatly beloved by the people of the north.

CHAPTTR XXII.

1. Now when the men of the south, found that they were beaten, and that not only was Stephen dead, but that Abraham was chief ruler, it came to pass, that they were filled with rage, and they spake unto James, after this manner;

2. —Behold, ye see what the north hath done unto us, in that they have rejected Stephen, and have made Abraham chief ruler,

3. —Also are we beaten in the matter of Kansas, and the soul of John Brown is marching on throughout the land.

4. Now therefore give ye us the possession of all the strong holds in the south, before ye cease to reign, for verily, it was for this that we suffered you to be made chief ruler;

5. Do this, and all shall yet be well with us, but if ye will not, then shall your life become a prey unto us, and we will put a man in your place that shall do all that we desire.

6. Then was James in a great strait, for if he did as they commanded, then would the government of a certainty be destroyed, and if he did not, then would these rebels destroy him.

7. For although James feared the men of the north greatly, yet he feared the men of the south more, moreover, his heart was with the men of the south, in all things.

8. But such was the watchfulness of the men of the north, in the Sanhedrim, that he was unable to do this, although in his heart, he greatly desired it, insomuch, that he wept, because he could not.

9. And when they saw that James feared to do as they desired, they called a council of the chief conspirators, and these are they that came to this council.

10. Jefferson, whose sir name was Davis; and William, whose sir name was Barksdale, from the province of Mississippi, (him that was aforetime put to shame, by John, called Potter, from the province of Wisconsin;) in the Sanhedrim at Washington;

11. —Lawrence, whose sir name was Keitt; Barnwell, whose sir name was Rhett, from the province of South Carolina; and Roger, whose sir name was Prior, from the province of Virginia.

12. Robert, whose sir name was Toombs, from the province of Georgia, (him that boasted himself so greatly, saying that he would call the number of his slaves at the foot of the monument, that standeth upon Bunkkers Hill.)

13. Lewis, whose sir name was Wigfall, from the province of Texas; and Raphael, whose sir name was Semmes, him that in after times, be-

came so notorious, as a robber, upon the great waters.

14. —Clemment, whose sir name was Vallandingham, from the province of Ohio; Gideon, whose sir name was Pillow; George, whose sir name was Pendleton; and divers others.

15. —Boasters, and braggarts all; but Roger, Lewis, Barnwell, and Robert, excelled all the others, in the multitude of the foolish sayings, that they uttered.—

16. Speaking great swelling words, against the men of the north, and against Abraham, and breathing out threatenings and wrath continually,—

17. — And that they themselves would never surrender, but would die in the cause, yea, in the last ditch; if driven thereto by the men of the north—

18. And although they sought it often, with tears, fleeing from one to the other continually, yet they found no ditch; that would hide them, from the wrath of the men of Abraham.

19. —Except, that of eternal infamy, in which all traitors find a grave, that seek to destroy the life of the nation, that gave them birth, and had placed them also in the post of honor, in her councils.

20. But in that; have they one and all found a political grave; out from which, for them, shall there be no resurrection, forever!

21. (For notwithstanding, that the government, have in their insane folly, restored many of these rebels to their former political rites,

22. —Yet will the infamy of their treason, still cling to them, as firmly as do the spots to the *lepro*, neither can any pardon, in any wise, wash them away.)

23. Because they lifted up their paracidal hands, against the best government the world had ever seen, and sought to destroy it.†

24. For not only had these men held positions of trust, and honor, in the realm, but they had also taken an oath, to be true in their alliegence thereto, therefore, was their treason the more damnable.

25. —Sons of perdition were they, one and all, full of all manner of wickedness, but Jefferson did excel them all in craft and villiany, and Jefferson did they chose for a leader—

26. And Jefferson counceled after this manner; behold ye see that although James feareth to do all that we ask, yet that he will in no wise do anything to harm us, for his heart is surely with us—

27. And but for the watchfulness, of the men of the north, in the Sanhedrim, he would surely do all that

---

†NOTE.—The clemency exte ded to the leaders, of the Rebellion, has never had a paralell, in the history of any other Nation. Tre son is the worst national crime that an individual can commit, and by the Law of every nation, in every age, has been punished with death, there never was a Rebellion more wicked or cruel than ours, and death should have been inflicted on every man, that had any active part in it, [as a leader.] These men expected to die, they knew they deserved death, and their contempt for a government that feared or failed] to punish [them], is greater to-day; than it was before they rebelled. And for this act of mistaken clemency, will God surely bring this nation to judgeme t. Neither will it in any wise escape.—The land is full of rebels, to-day, if not, what meaneth it that 6; southern m-mbers of the 44th., Congress, were unable to take the oath, provided by Law, at its opening Dec. 6th., 1875. Only 10 years, since these men were n arms against their country, seeking its destruction, and to-day, are in her council halls, as defiant as ever. Was ever folly like this?

CHAPTER XX.

we desire,—

28. Therefore let us take forceable possession, of all the strong holds in the south, before Abraham commences to reign.

29. For John hath not only filled them, with arms and munitions of war for our use, but Isaac‡ hath also scattered the ships of war, insomuch, that they cannot avail as against us.

30. Thus shall we get the possession of the government, and neither Abraham, or the men of the north, shall be able to prevent it.

31. And this council of Jefferson, pleased these rebels, and they exclaimed; great is Jefferson, behold he shall rule over us, and the north shall tremble at the mention of his name, yea, we will yet call the roll of our slaves, at the foot of the monument, on Bunkers Hill,—Selah.

32. And from that time forth, until the close of the reign of James, they filled the whole land with turmoil, and strife—

33. Yea, they even stood openly in the Sanhedrim, and defied the men of the north, saying; Abraham shall not rule this land, but Jefferson shall be chief ruler.

34. Now James, was powerless against these men, for he feared them greatly, insomuch that he counseled giving them all that they asked, even the possession of the government, but the men of the north would not permit it.

35. And when the ides of March were come, the reign of James came to an end, and he gat him to his own province, to a place called Wheatland, and he died there, and was buried, and no man mourned for James the IV.

36. For his reign was contemptible, and his memory shall rot, and his name shall be despised; of all the rulers of Columbia, he was the least.

37. Now the acts of James, and all that he did, and the folly that he committed, and the aid that he gave to the south,—

38. Behold they are written, in the Book of the Records, of the Sanhedrim, at Washington, made during his reign; and Abraham reigned in his stead.§

---

‡Toucy, Secretary of Navy.   §Lincoln, 1861.

CHAPTTR XXIII.

1. Now Abraham the I, was of the whig, or republican party, and like Saul, King of Israel, was from his shoulders and upwards, higher than his fellows, and from the province of Illinois.

2. And the men of the north, were greatly rejoiced, when he was made chief ruler, for he had never been sick with the rulers fever, was known to be a just man, and one that feared God, and hated iniquity.

3. Therefore did they say one to the other, surely is the hand of the Lord in this, for this man that we thought not of, hath been chosen, surely, it is the Lord, that hath done it,

4. And they gave him Hamilton, whose sir name was Hamlin, to go in and out before him, and to stand in his place in certain times; William, whose sir name was Seward, was chief scribe over the people; Simon, whose sir name was Cameron, was chief in the department of war; Gideon, whose sir name was Wells, was over the ships of war; Winfield, was captain of the host; and Salmon, whose sir name was Chase, was over the Treasury of the people.

5. And when the men of the south, saw that Abraham was firmly seated upon the throne, they were filled with rage, and their watchman blew the trumpet, saying to your tents, O, men of the south, for we have no part in Abraham, neither shall he rule over us.

6. And they gat them each to his own place, and made ready for the contest, for they were determined to destroy the government, and extend slavery once more over the whole realm of Columbia.

7. Now there was in the province of South Carolina, two strong holds, the name of the one was Moultrie, and the name of the other, was Sumpter, (albeit Sumpter was not yet fully completed, neither was it armed or garrisoned.)—

8. And they were nigh unto the city of Charleston, the chief city of the province, the inhabitants of which, were the worst rebels, in the land

9. And it was there that Andrew sent ships of war, in the days of John, called Calhoun, when he and the men of the south rebelled, for of a certainty, the chiefest sinners in the whole realm, dwelt in that wicked city.

10. Now there was a garrison in Moultrie, of three score and nineteen men, and Robert, whose sir name was Anderson, (a brave man and true,) was chief captain.

11. And the rebels had used much craft, and strategy, to obtain posses-

CHAPTER XXIII.

sion of Moultrie, and Sumpter, for they desired their possession exceedingly, but on account of the watchfulness of Robert, and his men, they were circumvented.

12. And when they could not prevail, they determined to take them by force, before they should be further strengthened—

13. But Robert divining their thoughts, again circumvented them, for knowing that he could not defend both, he left Moultrie, in the night watch, and took possession of Sumpter, because it was not only the strongest place; but it was also the most important—

14. For it was an exceeding strong hold, even one of the strongest in the realm, and had cost the people the sum of fifty score thousand pieces of silver, besides the arms and munitions of war it already contained, and that were yet to be placed therein—

15. (For it was not yet fully completed or armed, for which reason was it the more easily taken, for had it been completed and fully armed and garrisoned, it would not in any wise have fallen.)

16. Now on the morrow when the rebels saw what Robert had done, it came to pass that they were in a fearful rage, and they hastened to attack him.

17. And Jefferson commanded Pierie, called Beauregard, who was chief captain under him, saying: go ye up now against Sumpter, and take it; for we must have the place.

18. For lo, Robert hath betrayed us, in that he hath taken possession of Sumpter, and if we delay longer, it shall be that Abraham shall so strengthen it, that we shall not be able to prevail against it.

19. (Now Abraham had sent supplies unto Robert, but the ship* in which they were, was beset by the rebels, and compelled to return, and Robert was left destitute.)

20. Then did Pierie and his men environ Sumpter round about on every side, and when they had set the battle in array, he spake thus unto Robert;

21. Give ye us now this place, for we will have it, and if ye give it not, then will we take it.

22. But Robert said nay, ye cannot have this place except ye take it by force; for ye are rebels, and if ye attempt to take it, then shall we defend it with our lives—

23. Then did Pierie and his men, make war on Sumpter, on the twelfth day of the second month of the first year of the reign of Abraham, and took it, after Robert and his men had made a glorious defence.

24. And there was great rejoicing in the south, when this was done, and the men of the south said, surely is the Lord on our side, and we shall prevail against the north, and Jefferson shall yet be in the palace at Washington, in place of Abraham.

25. But when the people of the north heard that Sumpter and Moultrie had fallen, they exclaimed; would

---
*The Star of the West, sent with supplies April 5th., 1861.

to God! that Andrew was chief ruler, for then would these rebels not have done this, verily he would have hanged every one of them fifty cubits high—

26. And when it was known in Washington, that Sumpter and Moultrie had fallen, there was great indignation, and Abraham said unto his counselors, surely these men are fully determined to destroy this government.

27. Verily, it is useless to bandy words with these traitors, let us therefore go up against them, before they get too strong for us,—

28. And he commanded Winfield to make ready his army, even three score thousand, and fifteen thousand fighting men, and go up against them, verily, I will make them to know that there is a balm in gilead, and a physician there.

29. And Winfield did as Abraham commanded, and when the army was ready, he spake thus unto Irving, whose sir name was McDowell, one of the captains over thousands in the army of the north,

30. —Go ye up now against these rebels and destroy them, for ye are able lo, ye shall find them at a place called Manassas,—

31. Then went Irving up to Manassas, and they put the battle in array.

32. And the men of the north, were discomfited greatly, insomuch that they fled ignominiously, before the men of the south, even unto the city of Washington, the distance of twelve score furlongs.

33. Then was there great consternation in the north, for many had said, lo, we have only to show ourselves unto these rebels, and they shall flee before us—

34. While others in the north that sympathised with the rebels, (the same are called copper-heads,) rejoiced exceedingly, saying; a-ha! a-ha! did we not say unto you, that ye could not prevail against the south,

35. —Now therefore let them go, for ye ought not to prevail against them, neither can ye.

CHAPTER XXIV.

1. Now there was at this time in the City of New York, the chief City of the north provinces, a certain man, that wrote daily epistles unto the people, and who was also a leader in the affairs of the government, and had charge of the public mind, and great was the fame of him, in Columbia—

2. And the people had come to look to him for counsel, in all matters, that came before them, for they said, behold his wisdom is like unto that of Solomon of Old.

3. And he would oft times make a tour of the provinces, to instruct the people, in matters appertaining unto their morals, or religion, also in the affairs of the government, and the name of this man, was Horace, the sir name whereof, was Greely.

4. Now the parchment whereon Horace wrote his Epistles, was called the Tribune, (which meaneth,) to judge the people, and if any man committed any offense against the laws, then would Horace judge him in the Tribune.

5. And this he had done for many long years, until he had obtained great influence among the people, yea, he had even stood in the Sanhedrim, as a counsellor of the realm.

6. Now Horace was of the whig or republican party, and no man in the north, had said so many bitter things against the democratic party, and against slavery, as had Horace,

7. —And by the men of the south, was he more hated than any other man in the land, for the perpetual war he had waged against slavery.

8. Now he had great possessions, and like Solomon he built him a house, in the forest of Chappaqua, (the meaning whereof is) the place where one was lost.

9. Moreover, he had not ceased day or night, to warn the chief men of the realm, of the evils of ambition; saying that a desire to become chief ruler would bring them to shame.

10. Nevertheless no man in the land was more ambitious, or desired to be made chief ruler, more than did Horace—

11. Therefore came it to pass, when it was told unto him, that the men of the north had fled at Manassas, that it rejoiced him greatly, and he thought within himself after this manner;

12. Surely now is this my opportunity to become chief ruler in Columbia, in place of Abraham, by giving aid and comfort unto these rebels—

13. For peradventure, if I go over unto them, that they will forget all that I have done against them, in times past, and then by their help, (together with the copper-heads of the

north,) I can surely be made chief ruler,—Selah.

14. (For there were many of the democratic party in the north, that had joined hands with the south, and it was by their help, that the rebels expected to be able to overthrow the government of Abraham.)

15. Then did Horace give aid and comfort unto the rebels, in an Epistle that he sent throughout the realm, and he hastened to Washington, to counsel Abraham, as to what he should do, and he spake unto Abraham after this manner:

16. What is this that ye do, in that ye make war upon the south, surely ye cannot hope to conquer them, and if ye could, ye have not the right, for have they not the law on their side, it is better that ye let them go,

17. —Or if ye will not let them go, then shall ye pay unto them the sum of two hundred score thousand pieces of silver as the price of their slaves, for such is the law; better that ye do that than to have war.

18. And Abraham said unto Horace, art thou a teacher in Columbia, and knowest not that the thing that ye counsel, cannot be done;

19. —Verily, as the Lord liveth and I live, these rebels shall find that the way of the transgressor is hard,—Selah.

20. And when it was told in the north what Horace had done, the people said one to the other, what meaneth this counsel that Horace hath given unto Abraham, surely he must be looking to be chief ruler, or he would not have done this, and they were astonished.

21. Then Abraham sent for the chief scribe of the Sanhedrim, and commanded that he summon the members thereof, that they be in Washington, on the fourth day of the fifth month, and he did as Abraham commanded.

CHAPTTR XXV.

1. And when the men of the Sanhedrim were all assembled, it came to pass that Abraham spake unto them, after this manner:

2. —Behold ye see that the men of the south provinces have not only rebelled and taken Sumpter, and the treasure house in the City of Charleston,

3. —But they have also taken the treasure house in the City of New Orleans, together with the ships of war that were in those cities, and discomfited the army of the north at Manassas greatly.

4. Verily, if we bestir not ourselves, they will shortly possess the whole land, for every son of Belicl in the north is for them, and against us.

5. Now therefore let us get an exceeding great army, even fifteen score thousand fighting men, besides ships of war, and go up against them, for surely, it is nothing less than the destruction of this government, and the possession of the whole land, that will satisfy them.

6. And the men of the Sanhedrim, said unto Abraham, the thing that ye counsel is good, therefore, do it before these rebels get too strong for us,

7. Then did they get together an army of fifteen score thousand fighting men, for to subdue the rebels, and Winfield was chief captain.

8. Now Winfield, was a mighty man of war, even from his youth, and the victory was sure for the men of Columbia, when Winfield led them, for he was mighty in war.

9. But now he was four score years old, and could no longer go in and out before the people as in the days of yore, and he spake thus unto Abraham;

10. —Lo, if it please thee now, let thy servant retire from leading the armies of Columbia, for ye see that I am very old,—

11. Moreover, do I perceive that this will be a long and bloody war, for the hearts of these men are set on fire of hell, also are their leaders men of renown—

12. For Robert is chief captain; and John, Pierie, Sidney, and Thomas, are captains under him, all well versed, in the arts of war.

13. (Now these men had all been captains in the army of Columbia, and had taken an oath, to be true to the government thereof.)

14. (But in their madness had violated that oath, and were made captains in the army of Jefferson.)

15. Now therefore, choose ye a man to lead the armies of the north, that shall be like Joab of old, and he shall lead to victory, and Abraham said unto Winfield, where is the man

that shall do this.

16. And Winfield said; behold there is George, sir named McClellan, take him, and ye shall prevail, for he is mighty in war.

17. And Abraham said, the counsel that ye give me is good, and he made George chief captain of the army of Columbia, in place of Winfield.

18. And Abraham said unto George, behold ye are chief captain of all the army of the north, now therefore go forth against these rebels, and the Lord be with you as He has been with Winfield, and prosper you in all that ye do.

19. And George said, what thou hast commanded, that will thy servant do, only supply thy servant with men and munitions of war, and I will show these rebels that it is hard to kick against the pricks.

20. And Abraham said, the whole strength of the north is at your command, only be strong and of good courage, and the victory shall be for us, for the Lord shall fight for us, and against them.

CHAPTER XXVI.

1. Now there was a certain high place across the river called Potomac, that runeth near the city of Washington, the name whereof is Arlington, and it was distant from Washington about forty furlongs, and overlooketh the city, and the region round about.

2. And to this place did George lead his army, and he fortified it, and made it very strong, for he said, peradventure the rebels will attempt to take the city.

3. And he said unto his captains under him, make ye here now a camp, in which the army may be instructed in the art of war, for these men are unlearned in these things.

4. And they did so, and the army was instructed daily until they were versed in all those things, and it was called the army of the Potomac.

5. And it came to pass, when Abraham saw that the army was well versed in the art of war, that he spake unto George, that he should go against the rebels, for the people were very uneasy at this delay—

6. But George said nay, we are not yet ready, neither are these men yet able to go up against the men of Jefferson, for Robert is chief captain in the army of Jefferson, and he is a mighty man of war, even like unto Winfield.

7. Moreover, are not Pierie, John, Sidney, and Thomas, captains under him; behold his army exceedeth the army of the north in number, and they are also well versed in the art of war.

8. Wait until my men are well versed in all the arts of war, like the men of Jefferson, and then will I go up against them, and they shall flee before me, like as the hind fleeth before the hunter.

9. But Abraham said, go ye up now, for ye are able—

10. But George did not as Abraham commanded, but remained in that place until the first month of the second year of the reign of Abraham, to perfect his men in the art of war.

CHAPTER XXVII.

1. And it came to pass, in the first month of the second year, of the reign of Abraham, that he spake unto George saying; why stand ye here idle, go ye up now against these rebels, for ye are able,—

2. For hath not John, whose sir name is Pope, discomfited them greatly on the river called Mississippi, at the island called Number Ten—

3. And hath not Ulysses, whose sir name is Grant, put them to flight at the strong holds, called Henry, and Donaldson, upon the river called Tennessee, and hath he not taken those places,

4. And hath not John, called Fremont; and Nathaniel, whose sir name is Lyon, discomfited them greatly, in the province of Missouri—

5. And hath not Ambrose, called Burnsides, put them to shame, also in the province of North Carolina, and hath not the fear of him come upon every rebel in the land—

6. And hath not David, whose sir name is Farragut; and Benjamin, whose sir name is Butler, put them to shame, at the City of New Orleans, and is not Benjamin governor of that city—

7. And hath he not put a bridle in the mouth, and a hook in the nose, of those men that defied this government and boasted themselves so greatly of what they would do; yea, and are they not dumb before him—

8. And hath he not hanged William, whose sir name is Mumford, for insulting the flag of Columbia, and hath not the fear of him come upon all the inhabitants of that wicked city—

9. Now therefore go forward, and put them to flight, as Ulysses, and John, and Benjamin, and Nathaniel, have done, for ye are able.

10. Then did George march forth unto a place called York Town, in the province of Virginia, (for the rebels were encamped at that place,) and he cast up mounds against them, and besieged them.

11. Now it was here, that George whose sir name was Washington, overcame the hosts of the King of Britain, in the war of the Revolution, and took them all prisoners, therefore was it a notable place in Columbia.

12. And George, called McClellan, thought to do likewise with the rebels but alas, while he slept they fled away and escaped out of his hand, at which the people were greatly astonished.

13. Then said Abraham unto his counselors, George is not a man of war like Winfield, for lo, the rebels have escaped out of his hands while he slept,—

14. Moreover, I fear me greatly that his heart is not fully in this work,

CHAPTTR XXVII.

for when he is commanded to go forward, he saith, there is a Lion in the way;—

15. Now therefore, let us make Henry, whose sir name is Halleck, chief captain and he shall prevail, for Henry is able; and they said unto Abraham, it is well, so do lest we be wholly destroyed.

16. (Now Henry was not only a man of war, but he was also noted for his coolness and cautiousness, which caused many to think that with him for chief captain, the rebels would soon be destroyed.)

17. Then said Abraham unto George, this thing is too mighty for you, and you are no longer chief captain, but Henry, shall be chief captain,

18. But ye shall remain chief captain of the army of the Potomac, and ye are commanded to go forward and take the city of Richmond the chief city of the rebels.

19. Then did George go up against Richmond, and was put to shame, insomuch that he and his whole army fled for their lives, for the thing was too mighty for George,

20. For the rebels had set snares for him, and but for the skill and courage of some of the captains under him, would he have been taken therein.

21. And it came to pass, that when George did not take the city of Richmond, that Abraham was much displeased thereat, and he spake unto his counselors after this manner;—

22. Surely George is not a man of war, for he improveth not the opportunity, moreover when he hath it, he saith, there is a Lion in the way,—

23. For hath he not the whole strength of the realm at his command, verily it seemeth unto me that he could prevail against the rebels, if he would;—

24. Now therefore am I certain, that not only is his heart not in this work, but that he is for the rebels, and if left alone, that he will betray us into their hand.

25. Therefore let us put a man in his place, in whom we can trust, and that will smite the rebels, for the people are weary of this delay,

26. —And they put John, whose sir name was Pope, in his place as chief captain of the army of the Potomac.

CHAPTER XXVIII.

1. Now John, was a man of war, from his youth, was well known in the realm, had discomfited the rebels greatly in the west provinces, and the people had great faith in him.—

2. And it came to pass after he was made chief captain, that he wrote an epistle unto the people, and the army, in the which he boasted himself greatly as to what he would do unto the rebels, even more so than had George,

3. Saying show me where I may find them, that I may destroy them, for of a certainty shall they flee before me as in former times.

4. And it was told unto John, that the rebels were encamped at a place, called Cedar Mountain, and when he heard it he was glad—

5. Then went he up to Cedar Mountain, to fight against the rebels, and they put the battle in array, and John was discomfited greatly.

6. Now this defeat did so mortify John, that he refused to lead the army any longer, and George was again made chief captain.

7. —And John was sent to war against the Amelekites of the north-west provinces, and he did discomfit them.

8. (For the Amelekites of the north-west, had made war upon the inhabitants of the province of Minnesota, and slain great numbers of them, insomuch, that in many places none were left,)

9. —Inflicting cruelties the like whereof had not been done before in Columbia, but they were finally subdued, and one score and fifteen of them hanged at the strong hold called Fort Snelling;

10. —After which there was peace once more, in the north provinces between the men of Abraham, and these wild barbarians of the wilderness.

11. Albeit, their hearts are still filled with hatred against the men of Columbia, on account of the wrongs inflicted upon them in former times, by their fathers.

12. But after a short space, George was removed from the place of chief captain of the army of the Potomac a second time, and Ambrose was made chief captain in his stead.

13. And from that time George, sir named McClellan, had no part in the war, neither was he named among the worthies, for he was not a man of war.

14. Now Ambrose, was a man of war, and had smitten the rebels greatly in the province of North Carolina, moreover he was very zealous, and Abraham had great faith in Ambrose,

15. And when he had strengthened himself, he went up against the rebels, at a place called Fredericksburg, in

CHAPTER XXVIII.

the province of Virginia, and was put to shame, after which he like John, refused to be chief captain any longer, and Joseph, whose sir name was Hooker, was made chief captain in his stead.

16. Now Joseph was a man of war, from his youth, and was called by the men of the army, fighting Joe, on account of his great bravery and determination, for no man in all the army stood higher for courage than he;—

17. And the people took fresh courage, for they said surely will the rebels now flee before us, for Joseph is a man of war, even like as was Winfield.

18. And when he had strengthened himself, he went up against the rebels unto a place called Chancellorsville, and lo! he was put to shame, for the rebels were too strong for him,

19. Now after all these disasters, it came to pass that the people said unto Abraham, is there not a man in all the land, that can lead us to victory;—

20. And Abraham said unto them, peradventure there is such a man, but if so, the Lord hath not yet shown him unto me,

21. And they said, of a certainty Joseph is not the man, and if the Lord shall not show you such an one speedily, we are certainly undone.

22. And Abraham said, lo! George whose sir name is Meade, is a man of war, let us try him, and we shall prevail, and they said it is well, do so, and may the Lord give him the victory.

23. Then said Abraham unto George, behold I make you chief captain of the army of the Potomac, now therefore be thou strong, and of good courage, and peradventure, the Lord will work a deliverance for us, by your hand.

CHAPTER XXIX.

1. And it came to pass after George was made chief captain, that Abraham said unto his councilors, let us give these rebels one more opportunity to return to their allegiance to the government; for peradventure, many of them weary of the war.

2. And he sent them a writing, called the Amnesty Proclamation in the which, he certified them, that if they would return to their allegiance, that then they should have pardon, for all offences, except in certain cases specified in the Proclamation.

3. But they laughed at the writing of Abraham, saying neither will we lay down our arms, or return to our allegiance, but we will make a new government, in the which slavery shall be the chief corner stone.

4. Then said Abraham, behold, these rebels not only spurn our offers of peace, but they also openly defy the government; moreover ye well know that this war is for the extension of slavery over the whole realm of Columbia.

5. Now therefore, let us free their slaves, and then shall their chief corner stone be destroyed, moreover their slaves shall then fight for us, and against them, and our hands shall thereby, be strengthened greatly.

6. And this counsel pleased the people, and they said, do it; and then shall this crime of all crimes, and sum of all villainies polute the land no more, forever.

7. Then did Abraham make a Proclamation, and this was the writing of the Proclamation, that on the first day of the month, called January, every slave in the land of Columbia, should go out free.

8. Then was their great rejoicing in the north, and among the nations round about that loved Liberty, but the people of the south were filled with rage.

9. Then said Abraham unto George, ye hear the murmurings of the people at this delay of the army of the Potomac, also ye know that slavery is dead in the land; now therefore go up against the Rebels, and peradventure, the Lord will deliver them into your hand.

10. Then went George up against them unto a place called Gettysburg, and he fought them at that place, and put them to flight and their was great rejoicing in the north at this victory.

CHAPTER XXX.

1. Now the battle of Gettysburg was an exceeding great battle, even the greatest of the whole war.

2. For the rebels had been so emboldened by the several defeats of John, Ambrose, and Joseph, that they were sure of the victory at this time, also;

3. Therefore was it when they saw that the men of the north fled not before them, as in times past, that they were not only astonished, but greatly enraged also, which caused them to fight more fiercely than ever before.

4. But they could not prevail, for George showed himself to be a man of war, and they were beaten, and driven ignominiously from the field.

5. Now, not only was George himself a man of war, but the captains under him, were also men of war, and did valiantly for Columbia, in this her darkest hour.

6. George, whose sir name was Reynolds, (slain in the battle,) Winfield, whose sir name was Hancock; Oliver, whose sir name was Howard; Daniel, whose sir name was Sickles; all Captains of thousands, and men of renown.

7. And besides these was there from the province of Wisconsin, three valiant men, Captains of thousands, Lucius, whose sir name was Fairchild; Frederick, whose sir name was Winkler, and Lysander, whose sir name was Cutler.*

8. And to Lucius and Lysander, and their brave men belongs the honor of making the first assault upon the rebels, in this great battle.

9. Likewise, was there from the province of Wisconsin, that were not in this battle, Samuel, whose sir name was Fallows; Halbert, whose sir name was Paine; Thomas, whose sir name was Allen; John, whose sir name was Starkweather; George whose sir name was Bingham; Frederick, whose sir name was Salomon; and Harrison, whose sir name was Hobart.

10. Who for their bravery at Chattanooga, Allatoona, Chickamauga, Atlanta, Stone-river, Perryville, Mission-ridge, Antetem and other hard fought fields, were also made captains over

---

*Note—General Lysander Cutler was in many respects, a remarkable man, he was possessed of an iron will, and whatever he undertook to do, he would certainly accomplish, and although 60 years of age at the commencement of the war, yet no regiment that ever left Wisconsin, made a better record than did the gallant sixth. A better diciplinarian, could not be found, and regiments that were completely demoralized when placed under his control, were soon the best in the field. It was his firm hand and clear head, that made the iron brigade what it was, fearless as a Lion himself, he quicky infused the same spirit into his men. And under his command, they went into the battle, with confidence in their ability to conquer, with him to lead, he has gone to his reward in that would beyond the river. He was a true friend, firm for the right, and as firm against the wrong: surely while life remains the writer of this will never forget the happy day he has passed in the society of General Cutler, Peace to his ashes.—J. S. B.

thousands, and to John, and George, belongs the honor of being the first in the field, from the province of Wisconsin

11. Surely is there no province in the realm, whose sons marched forth at the call of their country, more promptly, or that performed more glorious deeds, for the cause of liberty, than did the men of Wisconsin.†

12. Now this defeat of the rebels at Gettysburg caused exceeding great joy, throughout the north, albeit their was great mourning also, on account of the men slain in the battle.

13. For so bloody had been this Waterloo, of the rebellion that one score and three thousand of the men; of the north were slain,

14. Nevertheless from that hour did the people take fresh courage, saying unto Abraham, surely have you now found a man that shall lead us to victory,

15. Therefore give ye now these rebels no rest, lest they get more help from the realm of Britain and became too strong for us.

16. For the people of the realm of Britain, had given aid and comfort unto the rebels, which had strengthened their hands greatly, for they not only built them ships of war, but they also gave them arms, and munitions of war in abundance—

17. Yea, and they gave them money also, wherewith to pay their armies; and did wickedly against the government of Columbia, with whom they were at peace, for they said surely shall the south prevail, and then shall republicanism be destroyed.

18. And George warred against the rebels until the fourth year, of the reign of Abraham; but he did not subdue them, and the people began to murmur again at this delay, saying wherefore does he not put them to flight.

19. (Now Henry was in fact chief captain but he came not into the field; therefore did the people call George chief captain.)

20. Verily if he delay longer, then shall we all be destroyed, for this war is becoming very grevious unto us, and they said unto Abraham. we are fearful that George is not the man for chief captain, for he pusheth not the rebels.—

21. Surely had he followed up his advantage at Gettysburg; by pushing the rebels, he could have destoyed them utterly — But like George called McClellan, he improveth not his opportunity;

22. And in consequence of this neglect, have they escaped out of his hand, and darkness begins again to cover the land.

---

†Note:—When the call was made for volunteers for three months, company A, of the first Wisconsin regiment was immediately organized with John C. Starkweather as Capt. George B. Bingham first Lieutenant, and Arthur B. Wheelock; was the first man to offer himself for Enlistment as a private, subsequently, however, when the regiment came to be officerd, Starkweather was made Col. and Bingham Capt. of company A. Went to the front, and at the battle of Falling Waters, first met the rebels, where George Drake was killed; being the first man too lay down his life in the cause, from Wisconsin. At the second organization of the regiment, Starkwheather was also Col., Bingham Major and finally Col. Vice Starkweather promoted, both are yet with us honored, and respected. Wheelock was after three months service commissiond as third Lieutenant of the Seventh Wisconsin battery, Capt Harry Lee, finally rose to the command of the battery and at the battle of Perkers cross-roads, did go od service for his country, was taken prisoner at Memphis, when Forest raided that place, and afterwards exchanged. Captain Wheelock is a man of giant fame, great bodily strength, and fearless, as a Lion. Married after the war, and settled in Dacota, and has become a man of prominence in that young State.

CHAPTER XXX.

23. Moreover, not only have many of our people been slain, but great numbers of them are prisoners, also, in the south and are treated with exceeding great cruelty.

24. For they are kept in pens like unto the beasts of the field, at Andersonville and at Bellisle, and at the City of Richmond, and other places in the south provinces.

25. Yea, and their keepers exceed even the Amelekites, and the Jebusites! who were the former inhabitants of the land in their cruelties, the like whereof hath not been done in any nation.

26. Verily if we prevail not speedily against these rebels, and deliver our sons from their cruelties, they will surely die.

CHAPTER XXXI.

1. And it came to pass at this time that the people spake among themselves after this manner;

2. Lo, now hath this war lasted four years, and it hath not only been exceeding bloody, insomuch that the whole land is mourning for the slain—

3. But the realm is also greatly impovished in money, and if it be not brought to a close speedily, then will utter ruin o'ertake us.

4. Moreover the time draweth nigh when the people shall elect a chief ruler, and the rulers fever is prevailing in the land, and George, whose sir name is McClellan; and John, called Fremont, are both sick with this disease albeit, John is not as sick as George.

5. And behold every rebel in the south, and every copper-head in the north, (and their name is legion,) is for George, for they say surely is he one of us, let us have him, and we shall have peace, which is all we want.

6. Verily, if George shall become chief ruler, then will all that has been gained for liberty thus far be lost, for he is surely for the south, and against us, and in Abraham is our only hope.

7. Now therefore, must we not only make Abraham chief ruler for four years more, but we must also find a man for chief captain, that shall lead to victory; for of a certainty the realm cannot bear this burden much longer.

8. And from that time on, until the ides of November, was the strife exceeding bitter between the men of George, and the men of Abraham, for the mastery;

9. But when the ides of November were come, George was put to shame, and Abraham was made chief ruler for four years more, and George gat him to his own place, and troubled the land no more—

10. For although he took of the southern remedies freely, also all the nostrums of the copper-heads of the north, yet it did not avail, for he had taken so much while he was chief captain, that it had lost its power to save.

11. And it came to pass after Abraham was made chief ruler the second time, that the people spake unto him after this manner—

12. Find ye now a man for chief captain that shall put these rebels to flight, for verily Henry is not the man, neither is George, for although he put them to flight at Gettysburg, still he doth not pursue them ;

13. And Abraham said unto them, where is there such a man, if ye know such an one, pray show him unto me, that I may make him chief captain;

14. Surely did I think that in George called McClellan, had the realm a second Winfield, but it had not, neither is Henry of any account as chief captain,

CHAPTTR XXXI.

neither was John, Ambrose, or Joseph, equal to the place, for the rebels were too sharp for them;

15. And now when we thought that in George, called Meade, we had found a man for chief captain, lo, are we again disappointed, for the rebels have circumvented him, also.

16. And they said unto him have ye not observed that Ulysses, whose sir name is Grant, is mighty in war, and that he smiteth the rebels continually.

17. For did he not overcome them at the stonghold called Donaldson, and at Vicksburg, and at Shilo, and he is moreover excellent in council, take him and ye shall prevail.

18. And Abraham said, the thing that ye counsel is good, and he summoned Ulysses, to come to Washington to be made chief captain.

19. And Abraham said unto Ulysses, behold, I have made you this day chief captain of all the armies of Columbia, and ye are clothed with exceeding great power, for ye are next unto me—

20. Therefore fear not, neither be dismayed at these rebels, but go up against them, and ye shall be sustained by the whole power of the realm—

21. Moreover, chose ye whom ye will have for captains under you, and ye shall have them, and take the army and go forward and subdue these rebels, for this delay is very grevious unto the people.

22. Then said Ulysses, this is what ye shall do, William, whose sir name is Sherman; shall be made chief captain under me—

23. And he shall take an exceeding great army, even five score thousand fighting men, and munitions of war in abundance, and go up against the city called Atlanta, which is in the province of Georgia.

24. While I with the army of the Potomac, will war against the army of Robert, in the province of Virginia, and then shall the rebels be encompassed before and behind, and these are they that shall be captains of thousands under me;

25. Phillip, whose sir name is Sheridan, a mighty man and true; Ambrose, whose sir name is Burnsides; George, whose sir name is Meade; Gouvernor, whose sir name is Warren; John, whose sir name is Sedgwick; Winfield, whose sir name is Hancock; and Franz, whose sir name is Sigel.

26. And Abraham said, it is well, thou hast chosen wisely, for these are all good men, and true, but Phillip is the greatest of them all;—

27. Yea, a lion in his strength is Phillip, giving the rebels no rest, but like as a lion teareth his prey, so doth Phillip the rebels, continually—

28. Therefore, hath thou chosen wisely, and now go thou forth, and may the Lord give you the victory.

29. Then went Ulysses forth from the presence of Abraham, and made ready, to do as Abraham had commanded.

CHAPTER XXXII.

1. Now William, called Sherman, was a mighty man of war from his youth, had already done good service in the cause against the rebels, was much beloved by the men of the army, and firm for liberty.

2. And he, like Ulysses had been taught the art of war, at the stronghold called West Point, in the province of New York.

3. For the government of Columbia, had established a school at that place, in which the youth of the realm could be instructed in all that appertained to the art of war.

4. And it was at this place that both Ulysses, and William, had been taught all these things, (at the expense of the people,) therefore did Ulysses choose William, for chief captain under him, because he knew him;

5. And Ulysses said unto William, behold I have chosen you, to be chief captain under me, because you are worthy, and ye are also clothed with exceeding great power,

6. Now therefore, choose ye whom you will have for captains of thousands under you, and I will appoint them.

7. And William, answered Ulysses, after this manner; George, whose sir name is Thomas; James, whose sir name is McPherson; John, whose sir name is Schofield; Henry, whose sir name is Slocum; Oliver, whose sir name is Howard; and John, called Logan; shall be captains of thousands under me; while Hugh, whose sir name is Killpatrick, shall command the horsemen.

8. And Ulysses said it is well, thou hast chosen wisely, for these are all men of war, and true—

9. Moreover, shall Hugh be unto thee as eyes, for he moveth with the swiftness of the wind, and hath the cunning of the fox,—

10. Yea, when the rebels think to destroy him, lo, he gathereth them as the husbandman gathereth his harvest, and destroyeth them utterly;

11. He leapeth upon them as a lion leapeth upon his prey, neither is there any that escape out of his hand, and the fear of him, and the dread of him, is upon all the south provinces.

12. A wall of steel, shall he be unto thee by day upon thy flanks, and a pillar of fire shall he be unto thee by night, to light thee on thy way, so that thine enemies find thee not.*

13. Therefore go forward and put these rebels to shame, and destroy that wicked city called Atlanta, that is in the province of Georgia, for ye are able.

---

*Note.—Killpatrick, was, as here described, a wall of steel by day, and a pillar of fire by night. The soldiers used to say, that they could always tell where he was in the day time, by the cloud of smoke from the burning houses, and at night by the light of his fires; for when opposed by the rebels, he spared nothing that would burn. Verily, was he, and his gallant men, a devouring fire unto the rebels.

CHAPTER XXXII.

14. And William, took his army, and went up against Atlanta, and fought against it, and took it, on the second day, of the seventh month, of the fourth year, of the reign of Abraham.

15. And he put the rebels to shame, and burnt the city with fire, and swept it, as with a besom of destruction.

16. And he marched throughout the whole province, and put the rebels to flight, scattering them like chaff before the wind, and took the city of Savannah, the chief city of the province.

17. Then were the rebels astonished beyond measure, and they said surely is our cause now lost, for these northern vandals, have taken the whole land, and our armies are powerless to prevent it.

18. For not only hath William taken Savannah, but Ulysses hath also taken Richmond, the chief city of the south.

19. And Jefferson, and his councillors have fled, and the army of Robert is encompassed by the army of Ulysses on the one side, and the army of William on the other side, and there is no escape.

20. Then said Robert, unto his captains, verily, we are in a great strait, for we are encompassed before, and behind, on the right, and on the left, by the armies of Ulysses and William, and we can hold out no longer.

21. And they said, it is better that we yield ourselves prisoners unto Ulysses, for Jefferson has fled, and Abraham is chief ruler for four years more, and our cause is therefore hopeless.

22. And Robert said, it is well for us that Andrew the I, is not chief ruler instead of Abraham, for then should we be lifted up above the earth,* (and justly too,) for surely our sin is great, but Abraham is merciful.

23. Then did Robert surrender himself unto Ulysses with all his army, and Jefferson was taken as he fled, in the apparel of his wife, by the men of Abraham, from the province of Michigan, and they shut him up in the stronghold, called Fortress Monroe.

24. Then was there great rejoicing in the north, the like whereof was never known before, and peace once more began to prevail in the land.

---

*Hanged.

CHAPTER XXXIII.

1. And it came to pass after the rebels had laid down their arms, that the men of the north said one to the other, lo! now shall the government be re-established upon a firm foundation, for of a certainty, with Abraham to rule, will the cause of liberty be safe.

2. Therefore, rejoice ye people of Columbia, for that slavery is dead, neither shall this crime of all crimes, and sum of all villianies, polute the land any more, forever—

3. And Columbia's proud banner, shall again be honored in all the realm, neither shall there be any more, a north, or a south, but the nation shall be one, and the people one, from this time forth, forever, Selah—

4. Well is it for Columbia, that such a man as Abraham is chief ruler, for he hath both wisdom, and understanding and will rule wisely.

5. And they gave him Andrew, whose sir name was Johnson, to go in and out before him, and to stand in his place in certain times, in place of Hamlin, for they said it will not only please the south, but the democratic party also (for Andrew was of that party,) and from the province of Tennessee.

6. And William, remained as chief scribe over the people; Edward, whose sir name was Stanton, was chief in the department of war; Gideon, remained over the ships of war; Ulysses, was captain of the host; and Hugh, whose sir name was McCullock, was over the treasury of the people.

7. For the Sanhedrim had made Salmon, a judge of the realm, even the chiefest of them all, for he was a mighty councillor.

8. And joy filled the whole land, because of the mighty things that had been done, and because the war was ended.

9. For the war had been very grievous unto the people of the north, therefore were they glad that it was ended.

10. But alas, this joy was soon to be turned into mourning, for a fiend in human form, whose heart was set on fire of hell, came upon Abraham in a public assembly, and took his life on the fourteenth day, of the second month, of the fifth year, of his reign.

11. Then were the people astounded, and they exclaimed, of a certainty these rebels should not be suffered to live, for their wickedness doth exceed all that was ever known before in any nation, verily, they polute the earth on which they tread—

12. Then was there great mourning throughout the north, the like whereof was never known before, for it even exceeded the mourning for George, the first chief ruler of Columbia, and the mourning continued, for many days.

13. And they carried Abraham, in great state throughout the north, that all the people might behold the body of their martyred chief ruler, and they buried him in his own city, in the province of Illinois.

14. Thus fell the great and good Abraham, by the hand of a rebel assassin,—George, the first chief ruler of Columbia, did well, for he delivered his people from the hand of the King of Britain, but Abraham hath done better, for he caused every slave in the land to go out free.

15. Then were the murderers of Abraham, put to death, and Andrew, the II, became chief ruler in his stead.

CHAPTER XXXIV.

1. Now Andrew the II, was a man of small ability as a ruler, full of pride, vanity, and self conceit, and for stubbornness, the wild ass of the desert, could not excel him—

2. Albeit, he had done the cause of liberty good service while governor of the province of Tennessee, in the war, and on account of this, had the people great hopes of him when he became chief ruler, but alas, they were sadly disappointed in Andrew II—

3. For it came to pass, when he became chief ruler, that he was exceedingly puffed up, speaking great swelling words, and boasting himself of what he would do—

4. Saying, am not I chief ruler in Columbia, in Abraham's stead, verily, was Andrew the I, a mighty ruler, and a mighty man in his day, and hath left a glorious memory,

5. —But the recollection of the reign of Andrew the II, shall never fade from the memories of the inhabitants of this land, unto the latest generation, Selah.

6. And when the men of the Sanhedrim spake unto him, that he should finish the work, that Abraham had begun, for the reconstruction of the south provinces, he answered them roughly, saying;—

7. Why speak ye unto me after this manner; am not I chief ruler in Columbia, and are ye not my servants, verily, did Andrew the I, chastise you with whips, but I will chastise you with scorpions;—

8. For behold, ye have nothing to do with this matter, but I will reconstruct the south, and whatsoever seemeth good unto me to do, that will I do, and there shall no man prevent me.

9. Then were the men of the Sanhedrim astonished beyond measure, and they said, what manner of man is Andrew, and what meaneth this that he saith unto us, ye have nothing to do with this matter, verily, he must be filled of new wine—

10. Now therefore as the Lord liveth, he shall find that we have something to do with this matter, and he shall moreover find that we are not his servants, but that he is our servant, verily, the first thing to be done, is to reconstruct him!

11. But Andrew cared for none of these things, and he defied the men of the Sanhedrim, moreover, he determined to make a tour of the north provinces, and speak unto the people, and also to make a pilgrimage to the grave of the martyr Stephen, that was in the city of Chicago.

12. Likewise did he think to explain the meaning of a certain writing, called the Constitution, unto the people, for he said, they be ignorant of its true

CHAPTER XXXIV.

meaning, notwithstanding, it had been fully explained unto them, in the reign of Andrew the I.

13. And he took unto himself, as councillors, men that were as foolish as himself, and the counsel that they gave, was like the counsel of Ahitophel, for they were of the foolish ones.

14. And one of these councillors spake unto him, that he should appoint him an high priest, who should go before him, and who should also write daily epistles, unto the people, (for they said,) lest they loose any of the words of wisdom, that ye shall utter.

15. And Andrew said, this counsel that ye give is good, and he made Petroleum, whose sir name was Nasby, high priest, and chief scribe, to go before him.

16. And he went throughout the north, and spake unto the people, and wherever he went, he made a shameful spectacle of himself, disgracing the high office of chief ruler of Columbia, and bringing contempt upon himself as chief ruler.

17. For he was filled with new wine continually, and spake like the foolish ones, insomuch, that the people were astonished at his doctrine.

18. And they exclaimed, alas, what manner of man is this, that we have made chief ruler, verily, he will bring us to shame, and they marvelled greatly.

19. Now the rest of the acts of Andrew, and all that he did while on his tour in the north provinces, and the disgrace that he brought upon himself, and the people, also the visit that he made to the grave of the martyr Stephen;

20. Behold they are written in the first book of the epistles of the prophet Nasby, and Andrew returned to Washington.

CHAPTER XXXV.

1. Now there was in those days in the Sanhedrim at Washington, three mighty men, men of renown; Charles, whose sir name was Sumner; Lyman, whose sir name was Trumbull; and Thadeus, whose sir name was Stevens,

2. And they were mighty in the councils of the people, for they had been long in the Sanhedrim, and had acquired great power in the land.

3. Now Charles, was from the province of Massachusetts, and was like John, (the old man eloquent,) firm for liberty, and he stood in the place of John, in the hearts of the people.

4. And Lyman, was from the province of Illinois, and was much beloved by the people of that province—

5. While Thadeus, was from the province of Pennsylvania, and was called the war horse of liberty, and these three were the leaders in the Sanhedrim, and among the people.

6. For they had great wisdom in all that appertained to the government of the realm, and the people looked unto them for counsel in all matters of importance that came before the Sanhedrim.

7. And besides these, there were also from the province of Wisconsin, two mighty men, men of renown, James, whose sir name was Dolittle; and Timothy, whose sir name was Howe.

8. And they were both mighty in word and deed, albeit, they had not been as long in the Sanhedrim, as had Charles, or Lyman, or Thadeus, nevertheless, they were counted among the worthies, but Timothy was the noblest of the two.

9. Now they were men of great intellect, well versed in all matters appertaining unto the laws, or the government of the realm, and they also had great power in the land.

10. Now James was in the Sanhedrim, in the reign of Abraham, and no man in all the north, was so bitter against the rebels, or did more by word or deed, in the Sanhedrim, or among the people, than did he.

11. For he was eloquent of tongue, and he went throughout the north, and spake words of counsel, and encouragement unto the people, which strengthened their hands greatly, and this he did do, all the days of Abraham.

12. But it came to pass, after the death of Abraham, and Andrew the II, had commenced to reign, that James, forsook the cause of liberty, went over unto the south body and soul, and became their champion.

13. For he had partaken of the sop, that they offered unto him, after which Satan entered into him, and he went out and betrayed the people, and the sacred cause of liberty into the hands

CHAPTER XXXV.

of its enemies.

14. Then were the people astounded, in that James had betrayed them, and they sent him a writing, that he should remain in the Sanhedrim no longer, but he would not obey them, for his heart was full of hate against the north.

15. But when six years were expired, the people said unto James, go ye now unto your own place, for you are a black hearted traitor against the sacred cause of liberty, and ye shall disgrace us no longer.

16. And they chose Matthew, whose sir name was Carpenter, to stand in his place, as a councilor in the Sanhedrim, and James went throughout the land to speak for the men of the south, and against liberty.

17. Yea, he even essayed to be governor of the province of Wisconsin, but the people said unto him, get ye hence, for we will have none of you, for ye are a traitor.

18. Now Matthew was a mighty man in the land, eloquent of tongue, well versed in the law, of a giant intellect, and like Timothy, true to liberty.

19. And the people rejoiced greatly, when he came to the Sanhedrim, for in Matthew and Timothy, had the cause of liberty two mighty champions.

20. And it came to pass, after Andrew had made his tour of the north provinces, in the which he brought shame and disgrace, upon himself, and the people, that there was great indignation, not only in the Sanhedrim, but also among the people, on account of it.

21. And they said one to the other, what new evil is this that has come upon the land, and what meaneth Andrew in what he hath done, verily, if he cease not this folly, we shall become a reproach unto all the nations round about.

22. Surely, he speaketh but the truth, in saying, that he standeth upon the Constitution, for he hath trodden it under his feet, verily, he must be filled with new wine continually.

23. And of a certainty, if left to himself, will he overthrow all that Abraham hath done, therefore this thing that is in his heart, to do, he shall not do, for we will prevent him.

24. For he hath shown us plainly by his folly, that he is not fit to rule this land, moreover, his heart is with the men of the south, and not with us,

25. Likewise, are his councilors as foolish, and wicked as himself, surely he cannot rule this land.—

26. And the men of the Sanhedrim, took counsel together, as to what should be done with him, for he set at defiance their authority, and would have none of their reproof, saying, that he was a law unto himself—

27. And one counseled after this manner, and an other after that, but they could not agree.

CHAPTER XXXVI.

1. And when they could not agree, Charles, from the province of Massachusetts, stood forth, and spake after this manner;

2. —A bridle for the ass, and a whip for the fools back, saith the wise man, verily, what Benjamin did unto the men of the city of New Orleans, the same will we do unto Andrew,

3. For his stubbornness exceedeth that of the ass, and his folly, that of all the men in the land, moreover, he is continually filled with new wine, and hath brought shame and disgrace upon the whole realm.

4. Now therefore, will we put a bridle in his mouth, and a hook in his nose, and he shall be made to know that he is our servant, and that he hath a master,—Selah.

5. And when he still defied the Sanhedrim, and anarchy had began to prevail in the land, Charles, Lyman, and Edmond, whose sir name was Ross, from the province of Kansas;

6. —And Benjamin, whose sir name was Butler; and John, called Logan; and Timothy, from the province of Wisconsin; took council together.

7. And Charles said, surely, when the wicked rule the people mourn, verily, this boaster must be humbled, therefore, let us impeach him and put him out of his office of chief ruler.

8. And this counsel pleased not only the Sanhedrim, but the people also, (albeit, Lyman and Edmond were the most zealous against him, of them all.)

9. Then did the chief judges of the realm, and the Sanhedrim, assemble at Washington, and summon Andrew, to come before them, to be tried for his offences against the laws.

10. But Andrew said unto them, behold, ye cannot impeach me, for ye have not the power, for there is no power in this realm that is above me, verily, you must think that ye are the rulers of Columbia, but I will make you to know that ye are not.

11. Then did they impeach Andrew, and when they should have prevailed against him, behold, Lyman and Edmond went over unto him, and the people were put to shame.

12. Then were the hearts of the people, filled with sadness, for they had hoped to put Andrew out of his office of chief ruler of Columbia, but Lyman and Edmond did prevent them, and there was great indignation in the north, on account of what Lyman and Edmond had done.

13. For they said, surely, our cause was just, moreover, we did prove him guilty, and lo, we are beaten.

14. What meaneth this therefore, for of a certainty, no man in the Sanhedrim were as vehement against him

CHAPTER XXXVI.

at the first, as were Lyman and Edmond, and they were astonished.

15. Then was Andrew more defiant than before, and from that time forth he filled the whole land with turmoil and strife, unto the end of his reign.

16. He also bartered justice for gold, took bribes, and practiced simony, and did exceeding wicked and foolish things against the dignity, and peace of Columbia, and his office of chief ruler.

17. Moreover, was there a certain Delilah,* in the land that overcame him, insomuch, that he denied her nothing that she asked, even to a place for one that was unworthy, or a claim that was unjust, until it became a disgrace to the whole realm.

18. Also he essayed to remove from places of trust, the men that Abraham had put in those places, and to fill them with men of low degree, and he brought

---
*Mrs. Cobb.

the nation to the verge of anarchy.

19. And when four years were expired, the reign of Andrew the II, came to an end, and he gat him to his own place, and troubled the land no more; and the people made Ulysses chief ruler in his stead.

20. Then was there great rejoicing in the north, that the reign of Andrew was ended; John, the III, and Millard did decieve the people, and James the IV, betrayed them, but Andrew the II, brought them to shame.

21. Now the rest of the acts of Andrew, and all that he did, and the shame and disgrace that he brought upon himself and the people of Columbia—

22. Behold, they are written in the book of the records of the Sanhedrim at Washiugton, called the impeachment of Andrew the II; and Ulysses reigned in his stead.

CHAPTER XXXVII.

1. Now Ulysses the I, was a mighty man of war, from his youth, and had led the hosts of Columbia to victory, and compelled the rebels to sue for mercy, therefore, did the people feel safe with him as chief ruler, for his wisdom in council was equal to his skill in war.

2. Moreover, was he a man of few words, not given to boasting, but a man of works, firm for liberty, of the democratic party, and from the province of Illinois.

3. And they gave him Schuyler, whose sir name was Colfax, to go in and out before him, and to stand in his place, in certain times; Elihu, whose sir name was Washburn, was chief scribe over the people; John, whose sir name was Rawlins, was chief in the department of war; Adolph, whose sir name was Borie, was over the ships of war; William, was captain of the host; and George, whose sir name was Boutwell, was over the treasury of the people.

4. Now Schuyler, was from the province of Indiana, had been long in the land, was well versed in the laws, and in all that appertained unto the government of the realm, and he was more beloved by the people, than any other man in the land, yea, even more than was Charles, for he was true to the cause of liberty; having never swerved from his allegiance thereto.

5. Also was William a mighty man of war, and was called by the men of the army, Old Tecumsche, for his craftiness, and was next to Ulysses in the hearts of the people, therefore, when the people made Ulysses chief ruler, they made William, captain of the host.

6. And the people rejoiced greatly, when this was done, saying, now do we stand on a firm foundation, and can rebuild what has been destroyed by the war, for Ulysses is excellent in council, as well as mighty in war;

7. Moreover, have we not Schryler, and Thadeus, and Benjamin, and Timothy, in the Sanhedrim, and are they not true men, and are they not also well versed in all that appertains unto the good of the realm—

8. It matters not, that Lyman and Edmond, have betrayed their trust, and joined themselves unto their southern idols, for they shall not prevail, neither shall the gods that they have chosen, be able to deliver them, from the wrath of an outraged people.

9. Then did Ulysses, and the men of the Sanhedrim take council together to see what should be done with the south provinces, and how they could be restored to their former rights, (except as to their slaves,) for they said, slavery

CHAPTER XXXVII.

shall never again polute this land.

10. For verily, was this war brought upon us, as a chastisement for this great sin, now therefore, will we have a law that shall forever prevent this great crime from again poluting the land of Columbia.

11. And one of the men of the Sanhedrim spake after this manner, saying;

12. Let us now make a writing, and offer it unto the people, of all the provinces in the land, and if it so be that the sum of two-thirds of all the people of all the provinces shall accept the writing, then shall it become the law of the land;

13. —But if it be, that the sum of two-thirds of all the people of all the provinces, shall not accept the writing, then shall it not become the law of the land.

14. And the men of the Sanhedrim, said this counsel is good, let us do it, and it shall become the law of the whole realm.

15. And they made the writing, and sent it into every province in the land, and this was the meaning of the writing;

16. —That every man in the realm of Columbia, should be equal under the law, both white and black, and the people ratified the writing, and it became the law of Columbia, and this law was called the fifteenth amendment.

17. Then was there great rejoicing in the north, among all the people that loved liberty, and great indignation in the south, and also among the copperheads of the north, and Charles, whose sir name was Eldridge; and James, called Dolittle; from the province of Wisconsin; were exceeding bitter against this law.

18. For the hearts of Charles, and James, like that of Clement, whose sir name was Vallandingham; were with the men of the south, and they did all that they could to help them, and also to strengthen the hands of the democratic party, both in the north, and in the south.

19. Now when the men of the south saw that the writing called the fifteenth amendment, had become the law of the land, and that not only was slavery dead, but that the black man was their equal, it came to pass, that their hearts were filled with rage, and from that time forth they became tenfold more the children of hell, than before.

20. For they banded together like the men of Jerusalem, in the days of Paul, and bound themselves with an oath, that they would take the life of every northern man in the south, if he fled not to a place of safety, and these men were called the Ku Klux!

21. And they disguised themselves, to look like devils, (which they were,) and rode throughout the land in the night watches, and took the life of every northern man, unless he had warning, and could make his escape.

22. For many had gone from the north provinces with money, wherewith to rebuild again the waste places made desolate by the war, and these men did they cause to flee, and return to their own land.

23. Then did the men of the Sanhedrim make a law for the punishment of these wicked men, called the Ku Klux, and Benjamin and Matthew and Timothy and others, worked for this law, but Charles from the province of Wisconsin, did oppose it.

24. After which Ulysses sent soldiers into the south provinces, and took these wicked men, and put them in the prisons of the north, and after this was done, there was peace once more in the land.

Note.—That wicked organization known as the Ku Klux, which sprung up after the rebellion was virtually ended, was the natural outcome of the spirit, that slavery engenders in the human heart. The object of this band of devils, was to accomplish by inaugurating a reign of terrorism in the south, what they had most signally failed to do by an appeal to arms, and was in fact a bold attempt to make the whole south a literal hell, [as far as the poor ignorant blacks were concerned,] shooting them down like dogs, as they did the white victims of their hellish rage, in that never to be forgotten place of horrors, that Ben Hill speaks so proudly of, Andersonville. Nothing in ancient or modern times, ever compared in devilishness and cruelty, with the crimes committed by this cursed organization. And yet the democratic papers throughout the north applauded and (with few exceptions,) defended it, yea, and are doing it to-day. Encouraged by this the south have succeeded in returning 63 of these fiends in human form, to the 44 Congress, led by that blatant rebel, Ben Hill of Georgia, for which the leaders of the democratic party, in the north are certainly responsible, as without their aid, and encouragement, these rebels would to-day be clothed in the garb of criminals, instead of disgracing the land that gave them birth, by spouting their treason in her Legislative Halls, and boasting of what they will yet accomplish. Think ye people of America of these things, for as certain as the sun shines, so certain are these men determined to get by votes, what they could not by force, and the north is full to-day of men calling themselves democrats, whose party zeal is so great, as to make them not only willing to do anything that such men as Ben Hill and his abettors shall command, to enable them to regain their lost power, but to pay the rebel debt as well, being in fact Ku Klux at heart, and would, if they had the courage, out herod Ben Hill himself in their folly and wickedness. Can a nation prosper that will do this, I tell you nay, the just punishment for all this folly is yet to come, *and come it will*, for what a nation hath sown, the same shall they surely reap.

CHAPTER XXXVIII.

1. And after this, it came to pass, that a great shadow came upon the land, for Charles, whose sir name was Sumner, who stood in the place of John the old man eloquent, in the hearts of the people, (and in whom they trusted,) betrayed that trust, and went over unto the south.

2. Then were the people astonished, and they said one to the other, alas! alas! what new evil is this that has come upon us.

3. Was it not enough that James and Charles, from Wisconsin, should betray the people, or that Lyman and Edmond, should prevent them from putting Andrew out from his place of chief ruler—

4. But now Charles, the mighty one, the lion of the north, who was never known to swerve from his integrity, or to falter, or waver in his work for the freedom and elevation of the black man, and for which cause was he beaten, even in the Sanhedrim with many stripes, must prove recreant also.

5. And there was great excitement and mourning throughout the north, on account of it, and it lasted for many days.

6. And there was also at that time in the Sanhedrim from the province of Missouri, a man, whose name was Carl, and his sir name was Schurz, and he also went over unto the South, as Lyman and Edmond, and Charles called Eldridge, and James called Doolittle, from the province of Wisconsin, had done.

7. Now Carl was from the land called Germany, that lieth beyond the great water, and had been a disturber in his own land, but had escaped from thence, to the land of Columbia.

8. Now Carl was eloquent of tongue, and desired exceedingly to be one of the mighty ones of the realm, but could not, for he was of an unstable mind.

9. And he joined himself unto the army of Columbia, and although made captain over thousands, yet he gat small renown, as a man of war.

10. But it came to pass, after Ulysses had conquered the rebels, that the men from the province of Missouri, sent Carl to the Sanhedrim.

11. Now the time again drew nigh, when the people were to elect a chief ruler, and the ruler's fever again prevailed in the land, and Horace, whose sir name was Greely, was exceeding sick with this disease—

12. And the men of the south rejoiced greatly, saying, surely hath the time that we waited 'for come, for Charles and Lyman and Carl, have come over unto us, Horace is sick with the ruler's fever, and Ulysses shall be chief ruler no longer,—Selah.

13. And they sent messengers unto Horace, to know if he would be recovered of his fever, (for it was sore upon him,) and the messengers came into the presence of Horace.

14. (Now Horace was at the house he had built for himself, in the forest of Chappaqua.)

15. And when Horace saw the messengers, he said unto them from whence came you; Trumble I know, and Shurz I know, but who are ye—

16. And the messengers said unto Horace, thy servants are from the south provinces, and we are sent unto thee, with a message from our master, and also to enquire after thy health, for thy fame hath reached the distant land from whence we came.

17. And this is the message that we bring unto thee, Jefferson, whose sir name is Davis; to Horace, whose sir name is Greely; sends greetings, health and length of days, be unto thee.

18. Be it known unto thee, that thy servants, who are men of the south provinces, were in former times the rulers of Columbia, and were exalted above all others in the realm—

19. For behold, we had men servants, and maid servants, and he asses, and she asses, and concubines, and although we toiled not, neither did we spin, yet Solomon in all his glory, was not arrayed like one of us.

20. But now are we in bondage to Ulysses, and the men of the north, and the bondage is very grievous, for they have spoiled us of our possessions, and we have become strangers and sojourners in our own land, and there was no deliverer.

21. And one said unto Jefferson our master, behold Horace layeth sick of the ruler's fever, at the house that he built for himself in the forest of Chappaqua—

22. Then was Jefferson our master glad, and he said unto us, this sickness shall work our deliverance from bondage, for as Horace did deliver me when sick and in prison,* so will I recover him, if so be that he will take the remedy.

23. For he desireth greatly to be chief ruler of Columbia, which he can not be, unless he get the remedy that groweth only in the south provinces.

24. Then said Horace unto the messengers of Jefferson, behold ye say truly, that my desire to become chief ruler is exceeding great, but tell me what is the remedy that ye will give me, and what will ye have me to do, speak for thy servant heareth.

25. And they said, come ye now over unto us, as Charles and James and Lyman and Carl and Edmond, have done, and ye shall be made chief ruler of Columbia in the place of Ulysses, and this is what ye must do—

26. Then said Horace if I do this thing peradventure ye will deceive me, as ye did Millard and Franklin, for ye did decieve them—

27. But they said nay, thy servants be true men, and if ye do this, ye shall surely be chief ruler, for with

---
*NOTE.—Greely went bail for Jefferson Davis, and was therefore in one source, the true cause of his being set free.

CHAPTER XXXVIII.

the help of the democratic party in the north, (and the liberals) we shall prevail, and they sware unto him.

28. Then said Horace, lo! my heart has been with you these seven years, that ye have been in bondage, for of a truth ye have done nothing amiss,

29. Therefore, whatsoever the men of the south will have me to do, (when I shall have become chief ruler,) that will I do, and there shall no man prevent me, and this is my answer to Jefferson your master.

30. And the messengers went out from the presence of Horace, and returned unto their own land, and when they had told the words of Horace unto the people, there was great rejoicing in the south provinces.

31. And they said one to the other, lo! now is the day of our deliverance at hand, for we have found a man that shall lead us out of this house of bondage, and we shall yet possess the gates of our enemies, and the men of the north shall again bow the knee unto us as in former times, Selah.

32. And they called a council to be held in the city of Cincinnati, in the province of Ohio, in the fifth month, (commonly called May,) of the fourth year, of the reign of Ulysses the I.

33. (Now, that council was called by the democratic party in the north, albeit, it was controlled wholly by Jefferson.)

34. And there was no man went to that council, that was not a disappointed office seeker, or a copper-head, or one that was ready to do anything to put Ulysses out from being chief ruler, for the next four years, if so be, by so doing they could get control of the government.

35. And Lyman, and Carl, and James called Doolittle, and Charles from the province of Wisconsin, with others as wicked, and foolish as themselves, did control this cage of unclean birds, for they had partaken of the sop, called boiled crow, that Jefferson had prepared for them, and their natures were changed.

36. Now these traitors were each unanimous for the man that the council should select for chief ruler, if so be that he was their man, but if not, then were they not unanimous—

37. And in consequence of this, was there great confusion when they came together, for Lyman was for Paul; and Carl was for Apollos; and James was for Cephus; and they could not agree.

NOTE.—The action of Mr. Sumner in regard to giving the ballot to the freedman at the time here referred to, has always been, and no doubt always will be, an enigma to his friends. Such a complete sommersault, certainly never occured before, in the political life of any of the great statesmen of America. It worked great and lasting injury not only to the poor blacks, but to the republican party as well, for had he stood as firm at that time, as he did subsequently for his Civil Rights Bill, Washington would not be full of rebels to-day. It was a sad blow to the hopes of the freedmen, for if there was any man at that time in Congress to whom they looked for help, and whose voice they had a right to expect would be raised in their behalf, certainly that man was Charles Sumner, no wonder they lost courage, when he betrayed them. But he has gone to his reward, and while we mourn his great mistake, we cannot forget the many years of warfare through which he battled for freedom, until like the mighty Daniel, [whose compeer in intellect he certainly was,] He succumed to the deadly effect of the White House fever and fell. But the nation will not soon forget that great northern triumvirate. The old man eloquent, Daniel, the God-like, and Charles, whose sir name was Sumner.

CHAPTER XXXIX.

1. Now there was at this time in the province of Massachusetts, a certain man, whose name was Charles, and his sir name was Adams, and he was one of the notable ones of the realm.

2. Now Charles, was the son of John, the old man eloquent, and was greatly beloved by the people, (but not as had been his father.)

3. And he was of the democratic party, nevertheless, he was a true man, and firm for liberty.

4. And when the council could not agree, they sent messengers unto Charles, for they wished to make him chief ruler.

5. Now Charles was at a place called Quincy, that lieth near the city of Boston, and the messengers came to Quincy;

6. —And one told him saying, behold there are certain men without, that desire greatly to speak unto thee, and he said let them come in—

7. And when he had looked upon them, he said unto them, from whence came you, for I know you not, moreover, I percieve by your raiment, and your speech, that ye are strangers in this place—

8. And they said, thy servants are from the council at the city of Cincinnati, and we have a message unto thee, from the council, and he said, deliver ye your message.

9. And they said, thus saith Lyman and Carl and James and Charles, come ye over now unto us, and ye shall be chief ruler of Columbia in the place of Ulysses, for verily, the people tire of Ulysses, and he shall rule this land no more.

10. But Charles said unto them nay, ye cannot make me chief ruler, for ye have not the numbers sufficient, therefore, verily, ye are like your father, the devil, for he did offer the same thing unto the son of man, if he would fall down and worship him—

11. —Moreover you like him, have no possessions to give, and whosoever trusteth in you, shall be put to shame, for ye are a nest of unclean birds, get ye out from my presence, for I will have nothing to do with you.

12. Then did the messengers return unto the city of Cincinnati, and tell the words of Charles, unto the council, and when they had heard them, it came to pass, that they were ashamed;

13. —And they said one to the other, verily are we in a great strait, for there will no man go before us in whom the people trust, and no man in whom they do not trust, can be of any avail unto us, for we are few in numbers, and they were in great tribulation.

14. And while they were yet in doubt, where they should find a man.

CHAPTER XXXIX.

one said, lo! there be messengers without from Jefferson, whose sir name is Davis, that desire to speak unto the council.

15. And it came to pass, when the council heard these words, that they rejoiced exceedingly, and they commanded the man that had charge of the door, that he bring them in.

16. And the chief man of the council said unto them, have ye any message, and they said yea, and he said deliver it;

17. Then said the messengers unto the council, thus saith Jefferson our master, go ye unto the council that is in the city of Cincinnati, and speak unto them these words;—

18. Thus saith Jefferson your master, this shall ye do, and it shall please me, ye shall make Horace, whose sir name is Greeley, chief ruler of Columbia, in the place of Ulysses—

19. For he is a chosen vessel to do my will in all things, moreover, have I prepared the way for you, to make him chief ruler.

20. And when they had heard these words, it came to pass, that their hearts leaped for joy, and they exclaimed with one voice, great is Jefferson, and they sent messengers unto Horace, at Chappaqua, (for he was still lying sick at that place.)

21. And the messengers came to Chappaqua, and his servant told him, saying, behold the messengers that ye have looked for from the council at Cincinnati, are without and desire greatly to speak with thee, and he said it is well, let them enter;

22. And the messengers came into the presence of Horace, and it came to pass, when he saw them that he sat up,

23. —And he said unto them, have ye tidings, and they said tidings, and he said speak, for thy servant heareth;

24. And they said unto him, thus saith Jefferson, and Lyman and Carl and James and Charles, behold ye are chosen to go before this people, and lead them out of this house of bondage, and now get thee up, and gird on thy sword, for the enemy is strong in the land—

25. Then did the heart of Horace leap for joy, and he said unto his servants, make ye now ready victuals in abundance, and kill ye the he goat, that I may make merry, for these men have brought me glad tidings of great joy;

26. Also, bring ye new wine and strong waters in abundance, for I perceive by the countenance of these men, that they be accustomed to use these things; and they did as Horace commanded.

27. And after the messengers had refreshed themselves, Horace said unto them, return ye now unto the city of Cincinnati, and say unto the men that sent you unto me, that when I shall have become chief ruler of Columbia, all things shall be as in former times, Selah.

28. Then went the messengers out from the presence of Horace, and returned unto their masters, and told all the words of Horace, and there was great joy in the council when they heard the words of the messengers,

and they hastened each to his own province, to have the people ratify, or confirm what they had done.

29. (For it was the custom in Columbia when a man was named for chief ruler, and it pleased the people, that then would they hold meetings throughout the realm to ratify, or confirm the choice, and this was called ratifying the choice of the people.)

CHAPTER XL.

1. But it came to pass, when Lyman and Carl and James and Charles, gat each to his own province, and said unto the people, come ye out now, and confirm what thy servants have done, for verily, we have saved the land from anarchy and ruin;

2. —That the people said nay, wherefore should we confirm what you have done, for Horace is not the choice of the people, neither shall he be chief ruler, but Ulysses shall be chief ruler for four years more, for he hath done well, wait ye until the ides of November shall come, and the people shall ratify you;

3. For is not Horace the friend of Jefferson, and did he not take him out of prison, when he should have been hanged—

4. And did he not meet also in council with Jacob, whose sir name is Thompson; and George, whose sir name is Saunders; and others that were traitors, at the Falls called Niagara, to consult as to how they might destroy liberty—

5. Of a truth the people of this land have done many foolish things, but this they will not do, Selah—

6. Surely, this realm hath not prospered since the reign of George, the first chief ruler, as it hath under Ulysses, and of a certainty, shall he rule for four years more, and ye cannot prevent it—

7. And who be you that ye take upon yourselves to make Horace chief ruler of Columbia, the people did not send you to the counsel at Cincinnati, neither will they obey you.

8. But like as Sanballat and Tobiah, did trouble Nehemiah, and his brethern when they would rebuild the walls of Jerusalem;

9. —So have ye and the men of the south provinces, troubled Ulysses, and the men of the north;

10. For when they would rebuild the temple of liberty, and strengthen the walls of the citadel thereof, and also build up again the waste places made desolate by the war;

11. —Then did ye like Sanballat and Tobiah, send out lying reports unto the people against Ulysses and his government, to the great damage of the realm, and also to your own hurt;

12. True you were once honored and beloved by the people of this realm, but alas! you are so no longer, for you have gone over unto the rebels, and betrayed the people, and sold your birthright, for the promise of a mess of pottage, and ye gat not the pottage.

13. Satan, (the first reformer,) was once an angel of light, and fell, ye were never angels of light, but ye have had a mighty fall, never more to rise again in this land.

14. And now get ye to your own place, for ye will never again be in power in Columbia, the people will trust you no more, for you are unworthy, and your places in the Sanhedrim, will they fill with men that will not betray them.

NOTE.—The defection of Doolittle, Trumbull and Shurz, at this time caused great astonishment in the north. No man in the north, had done more to sustain the cause of freedom, during the war than Doolittle. The writer was present at the great war meeting held upon the grounds of James Kneeland in '62, and heard this really talented man speak, and certainly no one of all the champions of liberty ever uttered more burning words, or execrated the rebels in stronger language, than did J. R. Doolittle. Wisconsin was proud of him, and justly too, at that time. But after Andy Johnson came into power, his whole nature was seemingly changed, and turning his back upon his former glorious record, he became the champion of the south, accompanying Andy in his disgraceful tour around the circle. And from that time forth, did his former friends and the cause of liberty, all the injury that it was possible for him to do. The reward of which treason he with Trumbull and Shurz, are now reaping. Having been buried in that political grave, in which it is to be hoped they will sleep the sleep that knows no waking.

CHAPTER XLI.

1. Now it came to pass, when Lyman and James and Charles and Carl, heard these words, and knew that the people would not confirm what they had done, that their hearts sank within them;

2. And they said one to the other, surely, these are not comforting words that the people have spoken unto us, verily, did we think it an easy matter to put Ulysses out from being chief ruler, and to put Horace in his place, but this looketh not like it, peradventure we have deceived ourselves—

3. For the voice of the people, soundeth like the distant thunder, that forewarneth the coming tempest, and unless we bestir ourselves, when the ides of November shall come, we shall be swept from the land, and the places that know us now, shall know us no more, forever.

4. And they took council together, as to what should be done, for they were in a great strait, and Carl spake after this manner, this people must be decieved, and this is what must be done.

5. James shall make a tour of the south and east provinces, and speak unto the people, peradventure he can decieve them, (for of a certainty hath he decieved the people of Wisconsin greatly;)

6. And Lyman shall go throughout the north and west, and speak words of wisdom unto the people, and **reform** them, for is he not the great **reformer,** and hath he not wisdom like unto **Solomon** of old—

7. For although the people have eyes, yet they see not, ears, yet they hear not (aright,) but it shall be, that when they hear the words of wisdom that he shall speak, that then shall their eyes and ears be opened;

8. —And they shall say one to the other, was there ever blindness like ours, for Ulysses hath brought this nation to the verge of ruin, yet we knew it not, and except for Carl and Lyman and James, he would have made himself king, verily, the people are blind.—

9. Then shall they come over unto us, and shall put Ulysses out from being chief ruler, for behold I, even I, do carry the votes of the people, that came from the land called Germany, in the pocket of my raiment.

10. And this counsel pleased these conspirators, against the liberties of the people, and they said let it be done.

11. Then did James make a tour of the south and east provinces, and speak unto the people, but wherever he went shame and disgrace awaited him, for the people said one to the other, behold who is this babbler;

12. —Is not this James, whose sir name is Doolittle, that betrayed his trust, and went over unto the rebels, in

the reign of Andrew the II, verily, we want none of him, for Judas like he, betrayed the people, but unlike Judas, he had not the courage to go out and hang himself.

13. And Lyman spake in the north and west provinces, but wherever he spake a chill came upon the people, and they said, alas! for Lyman, he was once great in this land, but what is he now, verily, is he and James and Carl, whitened sepulchers.

14. For although like the scribes and pharisees, in the days when the son of man was upon the earth, they outwardly appear like righteous men, nevertheless, they are inwardly full of dead mens bones;

15. —Working to put Jefferson and the men of the south, into possession of the government, but they shall not prevail.

16. And when they saw that they could not prevail, they compelled Horace to make a tour of the provinces, for they said, if he prevail not, then are we undone;

17. And when they shall have heard him, it shall be that they shall be convinced, for Horace is mighty in argument.

18. Then did Horace make a tour, and speak unto the people, and when the people heard him, they were astonished at his doctrine;

19. For it came to pass, that when he was come unto a city, and the inhabitants of that city did say unto him, what would ye advise, now if ye were chief ruler in a certain matter, (naming the matter,)—

20. That then he would say unto them, as your desire is, so shall it be unto you, for behold, I have no counsel to give you in this matter, therefore, whatsoever ye would wish to do, that shal" ye do—

21. And in like manner, did he speak, unto the inhabitants of all the cities in the land, in the which he did speak, to the great astonishment and disgust of the people;

22. Insomuch, that they said of a certainty, Horace shall not be chief ruler of Columbia, for he would bring more contempt upon us, than did Andrew the II, if so be that such a thing were possible.

23. But Ulysses shall be chief ruler for four years more, for if he is slow of speech, he is mighty in deeds, moreover the people do know what he meaneth, and that, like Andrew the I, what he saith, that will he do, but as for Horace, we know not what he would do.

24. And the contest waxed fiercer and fiercer, between the men of Ulysses, and the men of Horace, until the ides of November drew nigh, when the land began to be overshadowed by the coming tempest.

25. And when the ides were fully come, the storm of the long pent up wrath of the men of Ulysses, burst upon the men of Horace, and like the monsoon, it swept the land from one extremity unto the other.

26. And on the morrow, when the storm had passed, the men of Horace were not to be found, and the places that knew them once, will know them

CHAPTER XLI.

no more, forever.

27. Then did Lyman and James and Carl and Charles, put their hands upon their mouths and keep silence, for the space of three hours, for they were speechless;

28. —And when their speech came again, Lyman said unto Carl and James and Charles, heard ye any thing, and they said yea, and he said unto them yet again, saw ye the hand writing on the wall, and they said yea, we did see it—

29. Then said Lyman, verily are our days numbered, for we thought to deceive the people, but the people were not deceived, and now let us put our house in order, for the people will send us to the Sanhedrim no more, forever.

30. For we have not only betrayed the great trust confided to us by the people, in attempting to pull down the temple of liberty, built by our fathers;

31. —But we have sold our birthright also, unto Jefferson and the enemies of liberty, for a mess of pottage, and we gat not the pottage;

32. And the people have made Ulysses chief ruler for four years more, and there is no more a place for us in our father's house.

33. Neither will they kill for us the fatted calf, for we have taken our portion and spent it all in riotous living.

34. The wise man saith, truly he that diggeth a pit for another, shall himself fall therein, we digged a pit for Ulysses and his men, and have ourselves fallen therein, and no man will deliver us out of the pit.

35. Better for us that we had remained in our father's house, where there is bread enough, and to spare, and it were better for the people, that we had never been born, for we have been the cause of much turmoil and trouble, in the land of Columbia.

CHAPTER XLII.

1. And now therefore, all ye men of Columbia that desire to become great in the land, or to be made rulers over the people, hear ye the words of James, the son of Amasa, that he maketh Lyman, whose sir name is Trumbull, to speak unto you.

2. And if ye shall take heed unto them, and treasure them up in your hearts, ye shall become a blessing unto thy country when thou art called to be a ruler, but if ye heed them not, then shall ye be put to shame.

3. He saith: Seek ye not after the high places in the land, for gain honor, or for fame, for behold, what is honor, will it clothe thee; or fame, will that fill thy mouth with food—

4. And praise not thyself, but rather let another praise thee, neither seek thine own good alone, but the good of thy country, and thy fellow men, for in that is thy reward.

5. For behold, I was chosen by the people to stand in the high places, yea, even in the Sanhedrim, and was counted among the worthies, even among the mighty ones of the realm—

6. And it became a snare unto me, for I became filled with vanity, and I said unto myself, am I not exceeding great in this realm, who is like unto me, verily, there are none in this land that should be preferred before me;

7. Then was my head exceeding high, and I became filled with pride, and my heart was hardened, and I cared for naught but to get riches, and honor, and power, and to be exalted above my fellows—

8. Yea, I in the pride of my heart, even I, thought to be chief ruler of Columbia, for I was ambitious, and desired honor and fame, for my eyes were blinded to my own good.

9. Moreover, I got exceeding great riches, that my hands worked not for, but they gave me no pleasure, for they came not by honest labor, but they were the reward of wrong doing.

10. For I did stand before the judges, in the high court of the realm, and speak for the people, and take therefor a gift of ten thousand pieces of silver.

11. Moreover, I got my friends appointed to places of trust in the land, to the great damage of the people, for they were often unworthy, but I thought only to make my name great in the land of Columbia.

12. And I said unto Ulysses, appoint ye now my son governor of the province called Nevada, for he must have the place, and when he would not, then was my wrath kindled against him.

13. And I said if ye will not do this thing, behold ye shall be put out from being chief ruler, for of a surety whatsoever I want in this land that will I get, and who are you, that ye should say

CHAPTER XLII.

nay unto me—

14. Then did my feet commence to slide, and I walked not as in former times, for behold I was changed, for I had hardened myself to work evil, and to deal deceitfully, for I was jealous that any should be preferred before me.

15. Then did I conspire with James, called Doolittle, and Carl, and Charles, called Eldridge, and others as foolish as I, to put Ulysses out from being chief ruler, and to destroy all that the people had done, for the sacred cause of liberty and justice, for our hearts were set to do evil, and we were filled with rage;

16. And we did go throughout the realm, and become lying prophets to the people, for the evil spirits had entered into us, and we spake falsely, and worked deceitfully—

17. And now hath swift justice overtaken us, for our sins have found us out, and the people will send us no more to the Sanhedrim, but our places will they fill with honest men, that are true to liberty.

18. While we, like Cain the wicked one shall carry the mark of our infamy, and any that shall see us shall say, behold a traitor to the people and his country,

19. Therefore men of Columbia, that desire to be rulers in the land, join not hands with the unstable minded, or with those that seek their own exaltation, to the hurt of the realm, for the feet of such shall slide in due time, and there shall be no deliverer.

20. But when ye be chosen as a ruler, walk uprightly and humbly, before the people, for they are the masters, and thou art the servant, and it is for thee to do their will, and not thine own.

21. But if ye shall say as did we, who is like unto us for knowledge and wisdom, and what do the people know of these matters, surely we can deceive the people; if ye do this, ye shall put a knife to your own throat—

22. For of a certainty the people are the rulers in Columbia, and they are moreover not unlearned in those things that are for the good of the realm, and whosoever thinketh to deceive them, is not wise, verily, the people are not blind—

23. Moreover what will it profit thee to be a ruler, and have the people curse thee, and rejoice when thou art put to shame, and disgrace, for thy wrong doing—

24. Or, if so be that ye get exceeding great riches, even all the gold of the realm, what will it profit thee, for verily, thy food and thy raiment are all that you can enjoy, for beyond that it all is vanity.

25. For if ye had all the gold in the realm, ye could take nothing of it with you when ye shall go hence, and if ye could, where ye shall go (if ye have been an unjust ruler,) the fire would consume it all.

26. For verily the love of power doth contaminate a man, and the love of money, if a man watch not well his steps, will ruin his soul.

27. Therefore, when the people shall say unto you, come up hither, for we would make of you a ruler, whether the place be high or low, show thyself

worthy, for when they shall see that thou art faithful in small things, then shall they say unto thee, come ye up higher.

28. For the servant that doeth their will, the same will they exalt, but him that doeth it not, him will they put to shame, verily, the people are not deceived.

29. Therefore when ye shall be exalted to places of trust, deal justly and walk uprightly, before the people, for then shall ye prosper in all that ye do;

30. —But if ye do not this, then shall your feet slide, and swift destruction shall come upon you, for the people will thrust you out, and put you to shame, and ye shall be no more a ruler in Columbia.

31. And now hear the conclusion of the whole matter; Fear God, and keep His commandments, that thy days may be long in the land that He gave unto thy Fathers.

32. Then shall your life have been a blessing unto thy fellow men, and those that shall come after you, shall bless your name, and there shall be great mourning at your death;

33. But if ye do not this, then shall your name be despised, and your memory shall rot, for ye shall have lived in vain, and there shall be no mourning at thy death, for verily, whatsoever a man soweth, *the same shall he surely reap.*

Thus endeth the First Book of Chronicles of the land of Columbia.

APPENDIX.

The following thoughts have been suggested to the author while writing these Chronicles, as a fitting close to his work. For notwithstanding that slavery, which was the actual cause of the Rebellion, is dead in fact, yet the evil passions engendered on account of that, and the effort to place the black man on an equal footing with their former masters, still agitates the country. Which together with contempt of rulers, lust for money, and power, (and intemperance,) will, if not checked, ultimately do for us, what they have for every nation, viz: bring us to a speedy end, (as a Republic,) for of a certainty, for all these things will God bring us into judgment.

First, I will speak of corruption in office, and the contempt in which the people hold, and speak, of their rulers.

One cannot take up a paper in these days, but the first thing that meets the eye, is a charge of corruption, brought against our public men, stealing, bribery, simony, and every conceivable crime, of a public nature, is laid at their door. According to these journalists, our Halls of Legislation, (State and National,) have become cesspools of corruption. A state of things exist in this direction, that if not checked, will in less than one decade, bring this mighty Republic, purchased with the blood of our Fathers, in '76, and rebaptized in the blood of half a million of their descendants in the late Rebellion, to destruction.

Now in the name of all that is good, is this so? Are there no honest men in this great country, in public life, in our day? And have all the people become corrupt, and as the ministers say, totally depraved? I think not. But while claiming a small remnant, that have not yet bowed the knee unto Baal, truth, will also compel me to admit that as to the majority of our public men, (yea, and a large majority,) the charge is undoubtedly too true.

But whatever there is of rascality, in our public affairs, is due mainly to our system of elections. Good men will not become a party, to the nefarious measures, put in operation by the vile demagogues, and in too many instances demijohns, that aspire to an office or, a seat in our Legislative bodies. Consequently, our best men are seldom elected, and in consequence of this, are our Halls of Legislation too often filled with men of no ability, or moral honesty, but such as seek these places, wholly for plunder.

The lust for wealth, that has got possession of our public men, is also working great evil. Once $50,000. made a man rich, and there were few men in the land whose wealth exceeded that, consequently, no one man, or fifty men, could control the currency of the realm.

APPENDIX.

But now, $50,000,000. don't satisfy, and it is this love of money, that has so nearly destroyed what virtue, and honesty, there was in most of our public men, before they sought office But once in, and their pockets are soon filled with the people's money; stolen by the million, in the shape of land grants, Indian treaties, government contracts, and in fact, every conceivable kind of rascality, is put in practice to plunder the people, and what makes it look worse, on the part of the people, is the fact, that the more these villians steal, the more their victims, (the people,) seem to think of them, punishment not being thought of, except in isolated cases, where the thief has lost his political influence.

The lust for power, and the manner in which it is exercised by the great corporations that exist in this country, is likewise an evil of no small magnitude. A few men being able, on account of the vast number that are dependent upon them for employment, to send whom they please to the legislature, and of course procure through them, the passage of any law, that will tend to increase their already over grown powers, and weaken that of the people. There are too many Vanderbilts, Fisks, Jay Cooke's and Daniel Drews, in this country, these men exercise almost kingly power in the management of those mighty arteries of trade, that cover the land like a net, and whose gigantic folds, like those of a mighty anaconda, are fast crushing the life out of the people.

The subject of temperance, (or intemperance,) is also filling the land with turmoil and strife; and what a spectacle to contemplate The government of this great nation licensing the manufacture of—and receiving a revenue from—that which is filling the whole country with contention, vice, crime, pauperism, prison-houses, widows and orphans, and furnishing the courts, with a multitude of cases to settle, and criminals to punish, for violations of the law, in consequence of the manufacture and sale of this great curse of the human race. Every day do the papers give the sickening details of one, or more murders, caused by the use of this poison. And yet the work goes on. Will it ever stop? Alas! I fear me, never, and for this also, will God yet bring this nation to judgment.

But the greatest change, is in the religious world, so called. This is filled with agitation, as it has never been before, and to a great extent, old things have passed away, and all things have become new. We follow in the footsteps of our fathers no longer. They were humble, we are proud; they believed in a change of heart, we have more faith in the jack of hearts; they worshiped in humble temples, which they owned, we in gaudy ones, that some one else ownes; then a minister was settled for life, now they are never at rest, but with a few exceptions, they are continually changing, having no certain earthly abiding place; then ministers preached the plain truths of the gospel, for small pay and spared no one, now we get very little gospel for which we pay great salaries; then we heard very little dispute about creeds, now we have discarded all creeds, except that of making money; then we respected the faith and creed of our fathers, now we hold them both in contempt; then ministers blew the trumpet of the Lord, with a certain sound, now they blow their own with an uncertain sound. Would it not be well for us to pause, both in church and state, shut off some of our steam, go slow around the curves, before all that is worth keeping, in this land of the free, and home of the brave, shall have been lost to us, and our children, forever.

iv APPENDIX.

THE PILGRIM'S PROGRESS—
1620–1876.

1620. Lands on Plymouth Rock and sets up for himself
1621. Keeps Thanksgiving—in no danger of overeating.
1622. Builds a meeting house.
1623. Proclaims a fast day.
1628. Cuts down a Maypole at Merry Mount as a rebuke to vain recreations.
1635. Is crowded for accommodations and stakes o t a new farm at Connecticut.
1637. Makes war on the Antinomians and the Pequot Indians, and whips both.
1638. Starts a college, and
1640. Sets up a printing press.
1643. Goes into a confederacy—The first Colonial Congress.
1648. Lays down the Cambridge Platform. Hangs a witch.
1649. Sets his face against the uncommon custom of wearing long hair, "a thing uncivil and uncomely."
1651. Is rebuked for "intolerable excess and bravery of apparel," and is forbidden to wear gold and silver lace, or other such gewgaws.
1652. Coins Pine Tree Shillings, and makes the business profitable.
1663. Prints a bible for the Indians.
1680. Buys a "hang up" clock, and occasionly carries a silver watch that helps him gu ss the time of day. About this time learns to use forks at table; a new fashion.
1692. Is scared by witches again, at Salem, but gets the better of them.
1702. Founds another college, which at last settles down at New Haven.
1704. Prints his first newspaper, in Boston.
1705. Tastes coffee, as a luxury, at his own table.
1708. Constructs another Platform—t is time at Saybrook.
1729. Begi s to sip tea—very sparingly. It does not come into ami'y use til l five and twenty years later.
1710. Puts a letter in his first Post-office.
1720. Eats a potato, and takes one home to plant in his garden as a curiosity.
1721. Is inoculated for the small pox—not without grave remonstrance from his conservative neighbors. Begins to sing by note on Sundays, thereby encountering much opposit or , and opening a ten years' quarrel.
1740. Manufacturers tinned ware and starts the first Tin Peddler on his travels.
1742. Sees Faneui l Hall built. The Cradle of Liberty is ready to be rocked.
1745. Builds an organ; but does not permit it to be played in the Meeting House.
1750. Buys a bushel of potatoes for winter's use—all his friends wonder what he will do with so many.
1755. Puts up a Franklin stove in the best room, and tries one of the newly invented Lightn ng Rods.
1760. About this time begins to wear a collar on his shirt. When he can afford it, takes his wife to meeting in a chaise, i stead of on a pillion, as heretofore.
1765. Shows his dislike to stamped paper, and joins the "Sons of Liberty."
1768. Tries his hand at Type Founding—not yet successfully—in Connecticut.
1770. Buys a home-made Wooden Clock.
1773. Waters his tea in Boston Harbor. Plants Liberty Trees, wherever he finds good soil.
1774. Lights Boston streets with oil lamps ; a novelty [though " New Lights" have been plenty for some years.]
1776. Brother Jonathan—as he begins to be called in the family—declares himself free and independent.
1780. Buys an "Umbrella," for Sunday; and whenever he shows it, is laughed at for his effeminacy
1791. Starts a Cotton Spinning factory,

1792. Has been raising Silk Worms in Connecticut; and now gives his minister (not his wife) a home-made silk gown. Buys a carpet for t e m ddle of the parlor floor.
1793. Invents the Cotton Gin and thereby trebles the value of Southern plantations.
1795–1800. Wears Pantaloons occasionally, but not when in full dress. Begins to use plates on the breakfast and tea table.
1802. Has the boys and girls vaccinated.
1806. Tries to burn a piece of Hard Coal from Philadelphia. A failure.
1807. Sees a oat go by steam on the Hudson.
1815. Holds a little conversation at Hartford, but doesn't propose to dissolve the Union. Buys one of Perry's patent " helf Clocks," for $36.00, and regulates his watch by it.
1817. Sets up a stove in the Meeting House, and builds a fire in it for Sunday; an innovation which is stoutly resiste l by many.
1818. Begins to run a steamboat on Long Island Sound, and—after making his will--takes passage on it to New York.
1819. Grows bolder, he crosses the Atlantic in a steamship.
1822. Lights Gas in Boston. At last, learns how t make hard coal burn, and sets a grate in his parlor. Buys a steel pen [one of Gillott's, so.d at $33, per gross]. Has his every-day shirts made without ruffles
1825. About this time puts a Percussion lock on his old musket.
1826. Buys his wife a pair of queer-shaped India Rubber overshoes. Puts on his first false Collar
1828. Tastes his first toma o—dou't ngly. Is to'd that i is un ashionable to feed himself with his knife—and buys silver forks for great oc asions.
1832. Builds a railroad and rides on it.
1833. Rubs the first fraction ma ch—then called "Lucifer," and afterwards "Loco Foco." Throws away the old tinder box, with its flint and steel.
1835. Invents the revolver, and sets about supplying with it s a peacemaker.—Tries a gold pen, but cannot find a good one yet, nor t ll 1844.
1837. Gets in a panic—and o t again, after the free use of " shin plasters."
1838. Ad pts the new fash on of putting his letters in envel pes [a fashion which does not fairly prevail till seven years later.]
1840. Sits for his Daguerreotype, and get a fearfully and wonderfully made picture. Begins to blow himself up with "Camphene" and "burning fluid ;" and continues the pro ess for years, with change of names of the active agents down to, and including, "non-explosive kerosene."
1844. Sends his first message by el ctric telegraph.
1847. Buys his wife a sewing machine; in the vain hope that some how it will keep the buttons on his shirts.— Begins to receive advice from the " pirit World."
1855. Begins to bore and be bored by the Hoosac Tunnel.
1858. Celebrates th laying of the Ocean Cable, and sends a friend y message to John Bull. Next week begins to doubt whether the Cable has been laid t all.
1861. Goes South, to help compose a family quarrel. Takes to using Paper Mon y.
1861–65. Climbs the Hill Difficulty—relieved of his pack, after Jan. 1, 1864; but losses Great Heart, at the last, April 14, 1865.
1862. Builds a Monitor, whips an Ironclad.
1865. Gets the Atlantic Cable in working order at last, in season to send word to his British cousins, who have been waiting for an invitation to his funeral, that he lives yet.
1865–75. Is reconstructing, and talking about resumption. Sends his boys to the Museum to see an old-fashioned silver Dollar. Bores away at the Hoosac Tunnel.
1869. Crosses the country in a Pullman Car.
1872. Duns his friends, and advertises his business on a Postal Card.
1875. Commences to build for Centennial at Philadelphia.
1876. Holds Centennial.—*Hartford Courant.*

THE LIBERTY TREE.

A CENTENNIAL POEM.

The land of Columbia so large and so wide,
  Is the home of the brave and the free,
And here three hundred years ago,
  Was planted the liberty tree.

The pilgrims planted this glorious tree,
  On New England's rock bound shore,
While up from old Ocean, a pæon of joy,
  Rang out in its ceaseless roar.

Now in this generous virgin soil,
  This tree grew large and high,
Deep in the earth its rootlets ran,
  Where the nourishing waters lie.

But when old Albion's crafty king,
  Saw how this tree did thrive,
He gave command to cut it down,
  And leave no root alive.

For if, he said, it once gets root,
  In that prolific soil,
It soon our kingly rule will end,
  And all our plans 'twill foil.

For Albion's king, Columbia claimed,
  From east to western sea;
And swore that all who dwelt therein,
  To him should bow the knee;

But this fair tree still grew apace,
  In spite of George the third,
And soon its boughs became the home,
  Of freedom's warlike bird.

Now when this luny king, foresaw
  The people would be free,
To check this move he quickly made,
  A corner* on their tea.

For this new found Mongolian herb,
  That came from far Cathay,
Was used in seventeen seventy-six,
  Much as it is to-day.

Now George's Rex, was fond of gold,
  At least, that's what they say,
He therefore thought to scalp† awhile,
  In tea at Shawmut‡ Bay.

So quickly to that place he sent
  Three war ships large and tall,
Filled with this much loved Chinese weed,
  And offered it on call.†

He found no buyers at B. O.†
  Or S. O.† for his tea,
And soon some Indians came on board,
  And put† it in the sea.

Then did this baffled British king,
  Get in a fearful rage,
And sent his army to our shores,
  Under Sir Thomas Gage.

And thus this mammoth cup of tea,
  Steeped in old Shawmut Bay,
Brought on the war, that ended in
  Columbia's natal day.

One hundred years will have elapsed,
  In eighteen seventy-six,
When comes our first Centennial day,
  And shall it go for nix---

Nay, let Columbia's gallant sons,
  Respond to freedoms call,
And for this coming Jubilee,
  Make ready, one and all---

Come gather 'neath this mighty tree,
  That shadows all the land,
At the fair city near the sea,
  Where that bold patriot band,

Spake this young nation into life,
  By one decisive blow,
And said to Albions Pharo king,
  Now let this people go;

O! may our children ne'er forget,
  The day that made them free,
But every coming July fourth,
  Gather beneath this tree---

And as the ages onward roll,
  Though empires rise and fall,
On each returning hundred years,
  Hold a Centennial Ball.

J. S. BUCK.

---

*Board of trade term.
†Commercial Terms.
‡The Indian name of Boston.

TABLE OF CONTENTS.

CHAPTER.		PAGE.
I.	Gives a description of Columbia. Its discovery. The landing of the Pilgrims. With the reason for their coming. The War of the Revolution. The reign of George, the first Chief Ruler, and of his successor, John the I.	7
II.	The reign of Thomas the I. The purchase of New France. The war with Barbary, and Tripoli. The treason of Burr. The reign of James the I. The war of eighteen hundred and twelve. The reign of James II., John II. And the election of Andrew I.	11
III.	The reign of Andrew I. When Political troubles began to darken the land, in consequence of slavery, and foreign emigration. War with the Seminoles. And the Black Hawk War.	15
IV.	Continuation of Andrews reign. Trouble with the U. S. Bank. And its destruction by Andrew. Removal of the deposits. And the commotion in the realm in consequence thereof. Close of his reign.	18
V.	The characters of the first Chief Rulers, compared with those from Andrew I, to Abraham I. And the evils resulting to the nation from their unfitness. The unfitness of many of the Sanhedrim, by which the Government was brought to shame.	20
VI.	History of Ancient Albion. Hispanina and Gaul. With a short account of their wars, in, and on account of Columbia. And their present status among the nations.	22
VII.	Short History of the Welchmen, the ancient Silures. And their present status in Columbia.	24
VIII.	Short History of Scotland, the ancient Caledonia, her influence among the nations, and in Columbia.	26
IX.	History of Germany, the ancient Germania. And the influence the advent of her sons has had upon Columbia. Their manners and customs.	28
X.	History of Denmark, Norway and Sweden, the ancient Scandinavia. The manners, customs and religion of the people, past and present. And their status in Columbia.	30
XI.	History of Ireland, the ancient Hibernia. With a sketch of the manners, customs, habits and religion, of its inhabitants. And the effect their advent in Columbia has had upon its prosperity.	32
XII.	Continuation of the same, with a warning to the people, to beware of the machinations of the church of Rome, against the Public Schools. The head lights of freedom in any nation.	35
XIII.	Commencement of the reign of Martin the I. and the strengthening of the slave power, in consequence of his Political dishonesty, and moral cowardice.	39
XIV.	Continuation and end of the reign of Martin. And the election of William I.	41
XV.	Short reign of William. His death. The reign of John III. His betrayal of the cause of liberty. The close of his reign. And the election of James III.	43
XVI.	History of the election of James in place of Henry. And the cause of it. Eulogy of Henry. History of Texas. How it was settled. And possession obtained by Columbia. In consequence of the south compelling James to make war upon Mexico. The end of the reign of James. And the election of Zachary the I.	45
XVII.	Short reign and death of Zachary I.	49
XVIII.	Reign of Millard, and his betrayal of the north. The death of John. The fall and death of Daniel. The passage of the Kansas Nebraska Bill. Including the infamous slave bill. Close of Millards reign. Election of Franklin.	51
XIX.	Reign of Franklin. War in Kansas, commenced on account of slavery. Brutal assault upon Sumner, by Preston C. Brooks, in the Sanhedrim. The end of his reign. And the election of James.	56
XX.	The reign of James IV. During which slavery gained much strength, from his folly and imbecility. Occupation of Kansas.	60
XXI.	Continuation of the reign of James. John Brown's raid. His death, and its effect on the south. Rulers fever again prevails in the land. The north call a council at Chicago. Nomination of Abraham. Defeat and death of Stephen.	62
XXII.	Continuation of the reign of James. During which the traitors plan their attack upon the government. Death of James.	66
XXIII.	Abraham commences to reign. The rebels attack and take Sumpter. Call for 70,000 men. Battle of Manassas. The north defeated. And its effect on the people.	68

TABLE OF CONTENTS.

XXIV. Deflection of Horace Greely. Abraham calls the Sanhedrim together. Call for 500,000. men. 71

XXV. Winfield retires from leading the army. And George, whose sir name was McClellan, is made chief captain. Takes command. Abrahams charge to George. 73

XXVI. George makes a camp at Arlington Heights, in the which to perfect his men in the art of war. Is commanded to go against the rebels, and refuses. 75

XXVII. George marches against the rebels at Yorktown. Rebels escape. Henry made chief captain. George made chief captain of the army of the Potomac. Fails to take Richmond. He is removed. And John called Pope appointed. 76

XXVIII. John defeated at Cedar Mountain. George again made captain. Then Ambrose. Who is beaten at Fredericksburg. Joseph made chief captain. Beaten at Chancellorsville. George called Meade made chief captain. 78

XXIX. Abraham issues the Amnesty and Emancipation Proclamations. Battle of Gettysburg. Rebels defeated. And the rejoicing in the north on account of it. 80

XXX. Description of the Battle of Gettysburg. And its effect. Murmurings among the people at the tardiness of George called Meade. 81

XXXI. Abraham made chief ruler the second time. Ulysses made chief captain. Charge of Abraham to Ulysses. Sherman chosen chief captain under Ulysses, and is sent against Atlanta. 84

XXXII. Charge of Ulysses to William. He destroys Atlanta. His march to the sea. Lee surrenders. Jeff. Davis, taken. The war ended. 86

XXXIII. The rejoicing of the people that the war has ended, turned into mourning. The death of Abraham, by the hand of an assassin. 88

XXXIV. Andrew the II. commences to reign. Makes a tour of the north. Astonishment of the people at his conduct. 90

XXXV. Deflection of James called Doolittle. Matthew chosen in his place. Andrew and the Sanhedrim at war. 92

XXXVI. Impeachment of Andrew, when Lyman, called Trumbull, and Edmond whose sir name was Ross, from Kansas go over to him. Close of his reign. Ulysses made chief ruler. 94

XXXVII. Ulysses commences to reign. Passage of the Fifteenth Amendment. Ku Klux organised and their dispersion. 96

XXXVIII. Deflection of Sumner, and Shurz. Jefferson sends messengers unto Horace, at Chappaqua. Council at Cincinnatti called by the copper-heads, to select a chief ruler. 98

XXXIX. Council send messengers unto Charles at Quincy. His answer. And the selection of Horace. 102

XL. Attempt of Lyman, Charles, Carl and James, to have the people ratify the selection of Horace. And the answer of the people. 105

XLI. James, Lyman and Horace make a tour of the provinces. Horace defeated. Ulysses made chief ruler the second time. 107

XLII. The lament of Lyman called Trumbull, that James the son of Amasa maketh him to speak unto the people. 110

www.ingramcontent.com/pod-product-compliance
Lightning Source LLC
Chambersburg PA
CBHW020135170426
43199CB00010B/748